2015 EDITION

North Carolina Criminal Law And Procedure-Pamphlet # 19

Printed In conjunction with the Administration of the Courts

North Carolina Criminal Law and Procedure
Pamphlet Reference Guide

Chapters	Pamphlet
Chapter 1 Civil Procedure	1
Chapter 1 Civil Procedure (Continue)	2
Chapter 1A Rules of Civil Procedure	2
Chapter 1B Contribution.	2
Chapter 1C Enforcement of Judgments.	2
Chapter 1D Punitive Damages.	2
Chapter 1E Eastern Band of Cherokee Indians.	2
Chapter 1F North Carolina Uniform Interstate Depositions and Discovery Act.	2
Chapter 2 - Clerk of Superior Court [Repealed and Transferred.]	3
Chapter 3 - Commissioners of Affidavits and Deeds [Repealed.]	3
Chapter 4 - Common Law	3
Chapter 5 - Contempt [Repealed.]	3
Chapter 5A - Contempt	3
Chapter 6 - Liability for Court Costs	3
Chapter 7 - Courts [Repealed and Transferred.]	3
Chapter 7A – Judicial Department	3
Chapter 7A – Continuation (Judicial Department)	4
Chapter 7A – Continuation (Judicial Department)	5
Chapter 7B - Juvenile Code	5
Chapter 8 - Evidence	6
Chapter 8A - Interpreters for Deaf Persons [Recodified.]	6
Chapter 8B - Interpreters for Deaf Persons	6
Chapter 8C - Evidence Code	6
Chapter 9 - Jurors	6
Chapter 10 - Notaries [Repealed.]	6
Chapter 10A - Notaries [Recodified.]	6
Chapter 10B - Notaries	6
Chapter 11 - Oaths	6
Chapter 12 - Statutory Construction	6
Chapter 13 - Citizenship Restored	6
Chapter 14 - Criminal Law	7
Chapter 14 –Criminal Law (Continuation)	8
Chapter 15 - Criminal Procedure	9
Chapter 15A - Criminal Procedure Act (Continuation)	10
Chapter 15A - Criminal Procedure Act (Continuation)	11
Chapter 15B - Victims Compensation	11
Chapter 15C - Address Confidentiality Program	11
Chapter 16 - Gaming Contracts and Futures	11
Chapter 17 - Habeas Corpus	11

Chapter 17A - Law-Enforcement Officers [Recodified.]	11
Chapter 17B - North Carolina Criminal Justice Education and Training System [Recodified.]	11
Chapter 17C - North Carolina Criminal Justice Education and Training Standards Commission	11
Chapter 17D - North Carolina Justice Academy	11
Chapter 17E - North Carolina Sheriffs' Education and Training Standards Commission	11
Chapter 18 - Regulation of Intoxicating Liquors [Repealed.]	12
Chapter 18A - Regulation of Intoxicating Liquors [Repealed.]	12
Chapter 18B - Regulation of Alcoholic Beverages	12
Chapter 18C - North Carolina State Lottery	12
Chapter 19 - Offenses against Public Morals	12
Chapter 19A - Protection of Animals	12
Chapter 20 - Motor Vehicles	13
Chapter 20 - Motor Vehicles (Continuation)	14
Chapter 20 - Motor Vehicles (Continuation)	15
Chapter 20 - Motor Vehicles (Continuation)	16
Chapter 21 - Bills of Lading	17
Chapter 22 - Contracts Requiring Writing	17
Chapter 22A - Signatures	17
Chapter 22B - Contracts Against Public Policy	17
Chapter 22C - Payments to Subcontractors	17
Chapter 23 - Debtor and Creditor	17
Chapter 24 – Interest	17
Chapter 25 – Uniform Commercial Code	18
Chapter 25 – Uniform Commercial Code (Continuation)	19
Chapter 25A – Retail Installment Sales Act	20
Chapter 25B - Credit	20
Chapter 25C - Sales of Artwork	20
Chapter 26 - Suretyship	20
Chapter 27 - Warehouse Receipts [Repealed.]	20
Chapter 28 - Administration [Repealed.]	20
Chapter 28A - Administration of Decedents' Estates	20
Chapter 28B - Estates of Absentees in Military Service	20
Chapter 28C - Estates of Missing Persons	20
Chapter 29 - Intestate Succession	21
Chapter 30 - Surviving Spouses	21
Chapter 31 - Wills	21
Chapter 31A - Acts Barring Property Rights	21
Chapter 31B - Renunciation of Property and Renunciation of Fiduciary Powers Act	21
Chapter 31C - Uniform Disposition of Community Property Rights at Death Act	21
Chapter 32 - Fiduciaries	21
Chapter 32A - Powers of Attorney	21
Chapter 33 - Guardian and Ward [Repealed and Recodified.]	21

Chapter 33A - North Carolina Uniform Transfers to Minors Act	21
Chapter 33B - North Carolina Uniform Custodial Trust Act	21
Chapter 34 - Veterans' Guardianship Act	22
Chapter 35 - Sterilization Procedures	22
Chapter 35A - Incompetency and Guardianship	22
Chapter 36 - Trusts and Trustees [Repealed.]	22
Chapter 36A - Trusts and Trustees	22
Chapter 36B - Uniform Management of Institutional Funds Act [Repealed.]	22
Chapter 36C - North Carolina Uniform Trust Code	22
Chapter 36D - North Carolina Community Third Party Trusts, Pooled Trusts	23
Chapter 36E - Uniform Prudent Management of Institutional Funds Act	23
Chapter 37 - Allocation of Principal and Income [Repealed.]	23
Chapter 37A - Uniform Principal and Income Act	23
Chapter 38 - Boundaries	23
Chapter 38A - Landowner Liability	23
Chapter 39 - Conveyances	23
Chapter 39A - Transfer Fee Covenants Prohibited	23
Chapter 40 - Eminent Domain [Repealed.]	23
Chapter 40A - Eminent Domain	23
Chapter 41 - Estates	23
Chapter 41A - State Fair Housing Act	23
Chapter 42 - Landlord and Tenant	23
Chapter 42A - Vacation Rental Act	23
Chapter 43 - Land Registration	23
Chapter 44 - Liens	24
Chapter 44A - Statutory Liens and Charges	24
Chapter 45 - Mortgages and Deeds of Trust	24
Chapter 45A - Good Funds Settlement Act	24
Chapter 46 - Partition	24
Chapter 47 - Probate and Registration	25
Chapter 47A - Unit Ownership	25
Chapter 47B - Real Property Marketable Title Act	25
Chapter 47C - North Carolina Condominium Act	25
Chapter 47D - Notice of Settlement Act [Expired.]	25
Chapter 47E - Residential Property Disclosure Act	25
Chapter 47F - North Carolina Planned Community Act	25
Chapter 47G - Option to Purchase Contracts	25
Chapter 47H - Contracts for Deed	25
Chapter 48 - Adoptions +	26
Chapter 48A - Minors	26
Chapter 49 - Bastardy	26
Chapter 49A - Rights of Children	26
Chapter 50 - Divorce and Alimony	26
Chapter 50A - Uniform Child-Custody Jurisdiction and	

Enforcement Act	26
Chapter 50B - Domestic Violence	26
Chapter 50C - Civil No-Contact Orders	26
Chapter 51 - Marriage	26
Chapter 52 - Powers and Liabilities of Married Persons	27
Chapter 52A - Uniform Reciprocal Enforcement of Support Act [Repealed.]	27
Chapter 52B - Uniform Premarital Agreement Act	27
Chapter 52C - Uniform Interstate Family Support Act	27
Chapter 53 - Banks	27
Chapter 53A - Business Development Corporations and North Carolina Capital Resource Corporations	28
Chapter 53B - Financial Privacy Act	28
Chapter 54 - Cooperative Organizations	28
Chapter 54A - Capital Stock Savings and Loan Associations [Repealed.]	28
Chapter 54B - Savings and Loan Associations	29
Chapter 54C - Savings Banks	29
Chapter 55 - North Carolina Business Corporation Act	30
Chapter 55A - North Carolina Nonprofit Corporation Act	31
Chapter 55B - Professional Corporation Act	31
Chapter 55C - Foreign Trade Zones	31
Chapter 55D - Filings, Names, and Registered Agents for Corporations, Nonprofit Corporations, and Partnerships	31
Chapter 56 - Electric, Telegraph and Power Companies [Repealed.]	31
Chapter 57 - Hospital, Medical and Dental Service Corporations [Recodified.]	31
Chapter 57A - Health Maintenance Organization Act [Recodified.]	31
Chapter 57B - Health Maintenance Organization Act [Recodified.]	31
Chapter 57C - North Carolina Limited Liability Company Act.	31
Chapter 58 - Insurance	32
Chapter 58 - Insurance (Continuation)	33
Chapter 58 - Insurance (Continuation)	34
Chapter 58 - Insurance (Continuation)	35
Chapter 58 - Insurance (Continuation)	36
Chapter 58 - Insurance (Continuation)	37
Chapter 58 - Insurance (Continuation)	38
Chapter 58A - North Carolina Health Insurance Trust Commission [Recodified.]	38
Chapter 59 - Partnership.	39
Chapter 59B - Uniform Unincorporated Nonprofit Association Act.	39
Chapter 60 - Railroads and Other Carriers [Repealed and Transferred.]	39
Chapter 61 - Religious Societies	39
Chapter 62 - Public Utilities	39

Chapter 62 - Public Utilities (Continuation)	40
Chapter 62A - Public Safety Telephone Service And Wireless Telephone Service	40
Chapter 63 - Aeronautics	40
Chapter 63A - North Carolina Global TransPark Authority	40
Chapter 64 - Aliens	40
Chapter 65 – Cemeteries	40
Chapter 66 - Commerce and Business	41
Chapter 67 - Dogs	41
Chapter 68 - Fences and Stock Law	41
Chapter 69 - Fire Protection	41
Chapter 70 - Indian Antiquities, Archaeological Resources and Unmarked Human Skeletal Remains Protection	42
Chapter 71 - Indians [Repealed.]	42
Chapter 71A - Indians	42
Chapter 72 - Inns, Hotels and Restaurants	42
Chapter 73 - Mills	42
Chapter 74 - Mines and Quarries	42
Chapter 74A - Company Police [Repealed.]	42
Chapter 74B - Private Protective Services Act [Repealed.]	42
Chapter 74C - Private Protective Services	42
Chapter 74D - Alarm Systems	42
Chapter 74E - Company Police Act	42
Chapter 74F - Locksmith Licensing Act	42
Chapter 74G - Campus Police Act	42
Chapter 75 - Monopolies, Trusts and Consumer Protection	42
Chapter 75A - Boating and Water Safety	43
Chapter 75B - Discrimination in Business	43
Chapter 75C - Motion Picture Fair Competition Act	43
Chapter 75D - Racketeer Influenced and Corrupt Organizations	43
Chapter 75E - Unlawful Activities in Connection With Certain Corporate Transactions	43
Chapter 76 - Navigation	43
Chapter 76A - Navigation and Pilotage Commissions	43
Chapter 77 - Rivers, Creeks, and Coastal Waters	43
Chapter 78 - Securities Law [Repealed.]	43
Chapter 78A - North Carolina Securities Act	43
Chapter 78B - Tender Offer Disclosure Act [Repealed.]	43
Chapter 78C - Investment Advisers	43
Chapter 78D - Commodities Act	43
Chapter 79 - Strays [Repealed.]	43
Chapter 80 - Trademarks, Brands, etc.	44
Chapter 81 - Weights and Measures [Recodified.]	44
Chapter 81A - Weights and Measures Act of 1975.	44
Chapter 82 - Wrecks [Repealed.]	44
Chapter 83 - Architects [Recodified.]	44

Chapter 83A - Architects	44
Chapter 84 - Attorneys-at-Law	44
Chapter 84A - Foreign Legal Consultants	44
Chapter 85 - Auctions and Auctioneers [Repealed.]	44
Chapter 85A - Bail Bondsmen and Runners [Recodified.]	44
Chapter 85B - Auctions and Auctioneers	44
Chapter 85C - Bail Bondsmen and Runners [Recodified.]	44
Chapter 86 - Barbers [Recodified.]	44
Chapter 86A - Barbers	44
Chapter 87 - Contractors	44
Chapter 88 - Cosmetic Art [Repealed.]	44
Chapter 88A - Electrolysis Practice Act	44
Chapter 88B - Cosmetic Art	45
Chapter 89 - Engineering and Land Surveying [Recodified.]	45
Chapter 89A - Landscape Architects	45
Chapter 89B - Foresters	45
Chapter 89C - Engineering and Land Surveying	45
Chapter 89D - Landscape Contractors	45
Chapter 89E - Geologists Licensing Act	45
Chapter 89F - North Carolina Soil Scientist Licensing Act	45
Chapter 89G - Irrigation Contractors	45
Chapter 90 - Medicine and Allied Occupations	45
Chapter 90 - Medicine and Allied Occupations (Continuation)	46
Chapter 90 - Medicine and Allied Occupations (Continuation)	47
Chapter 90 - Medicine and Allied Occupations (Continuation)	48
Chapter 90A - Sanitarians and Water and Wastewater Treatment Facility Operators	48
Chapter 90B - Social Worker Certification and Licensure Act	48
Chapter 90C - North Carolina Recreational Therapy Licensure Act	48
Chapter 90D - Interpreters and Transliterators	48
Chapter 91 - Pawnbrokers [Repealed.]	48
Chapter 91A - Pawnbrokers Modernization Act of 1989	48
Chapter 92 - Photographers [Deleted.]	48
Chapter 93 - Certified Public Accountants	48
Chapter 93A - Real Estate License Law	49
Chapter 93B - Occupational Licensing Boards	49
Chapter 93C - Watchmakers [Repealed.]	49
Chapter 93D - North Carolina State Hearing Aid Dealers and Fitters Board.	49
Chapter 93E - North Carolina Appraisers Act	49
Chapter 94 - Apprenticeship	49
Chapter 95 - Department of Labor and Labor Regulations	49
Chapter 95 - Department of Labor and Labor Regulations (Continuation)	50
Chapter 96 - Employment Security	50
Chapter 97 - Workers' Compensation Act	50
Chapter 97 - Workers' Compensation Act (Continuation)	51

Chapter 98 - Burnt and Lost Records	51
Chapter 99 - Libel and Slander	51
Chapter 99A - Civil Remedies for Criminal Actions	51
Chapter 99B - Products Liability	51
Chapter 99C - Actions Relating to Winter Sports Safety and Accidents	51
Chapter 99D - Civil Rights	51
Chapter 99E - Special Liability Provisions	51
Chapter 100 - Monuments, Memorials and Parks	51
Chapter 101 - Names of Persons	51
Chapter 102 - Official Survey Base	51
Chapter 103 - Sundays, Holidays and Special Days	51
Chapter 104 - United States Lands	51
Chapter 104A - Degrees of Kinship	51
Chapter 104B - Hurricanes or Other Acts of Nature	51
Chapter 104C - Atomic Energy, Radioactivity and Ionizing Radiation [Repealed and Recodified.]	51
Chapter 104D - Southern States Energy Compact	51
Chapter 104E - North Carolina Radiation Protection Act	51
Chapter 104F - Southeast Interstate Low-Level Radioactive Waste Management Compact [Repealed]	51
Chapter 104G - North Carolina Low-Level Radioactive Waste Management Authority Act of 1987 [Repealed]	51
Chapter 105 - Taxation	51
Chapter 105 - Taxation (Continuation)	52
Chapter 105 - Taxation (Continuation)	53
Chapter 105 - Taxation (Continuation)	54
Chapter 105A - Setoff Debt Collection Act	55
Chapter 105B - Defaulted Student Loan Recovery Act	55
Chapter 106 - Agriculture	55
Chapter 106 - Agriculture (Continue)	56
Chapter 106 - Agriculture (Continue)	57
Chapter 107 - Agricultural Development Districts [Repealed.]	57
Chapter 108 - Social Services [Repealed and Recodified.]	57
Chapter 108A - Social Services	57
Chapter 108B - Community Action Programs	58
Chapter 108C Medicaid and Health Choice Provider Requirements.	58
Chapter 108D Medicaid Managed Care for Behavioral Health Services.	58
Chapter 109 - Bonds [Recodified.]	58
Chapter 110 - Child Welfare	58
Chapter 111 - Aid to the Blind	58
Chapter 112 - Confederate Homes and Pensions [Repealed.]	58
Chapter 113 - Conservation and Development	58
Chapter 113 - Conservation and Development (Continuation)	59

Chapter 113A - Pollution Control and Environment	59
Chapter 113A - Pollution Control and Environment (Continuation)	60
Chapter 113B - North Carolina Energy Policy Act of 1975	60
Chapter 114 - Department of Justice	60
Chapter 115 - Elementary and Secondary Education [Repealed.]	60
Chapter 115A - Community Colleges, Technical Institutes, and Industrial Education Centers [Repealed.]	60
Chapter 115B - Tuition and Fee Waivers	60
Chapter 115C - Elementary and Secondary Education	60
Chapter 115C - Elementary and Secondary Education (Continuation)	61
Chapter 115C - Elementary and Secondary Education (Continuation)	62
Chapter 115C - Elementary and Secondary Education (Continuation)	63
Chapter 115D - Community Colleges	63
Chapter 115E - Private Educational Facilities Finance Act [Recodified]	63
Chapter 116 - Higher Education	63
Chapter 116 - Higher Education (Continuation)	63
Chapter 116A - Escheats and Abandoned Property [Repealed.]	64
Chapter 116B - Escheats and Abandoned Property	64
Chapter 116C - Continuum of Education Programs	64
Chapter 116D - Higher Education Bonds	64
Chapter 117 - Electrification	64
Chapter 118 - Firemen's and Rescue Squad Workers' Relief and Pension Funds [Recodified.]	64
Chapter 118A - Firemen's Death Benefit Act [Repealed.]	64
Chapter 118B - Members of a Rescue Squad Death Benefit Act [Repealed.]	64
Chapter 119 - Gasoline and Oil Inspection and Regulation	64
Chapter 120 - General Assembly	65
Chapter 120 - General Assembly (Continuation)	66
Chapter 120 - General Assembly (Continuation)	67
Chapter 120C - Lobbying	67
Chapter 121 - Archives and History	67
Chapter 122 - Hospitals for the Mentally Disordered [Repealed.]	67
Chapter 122A - North Carolina Housing Finance Agency	67
Chapter 122B - North Carolina Agricultural Facilities Finance Act [Repealed.]	67
Chapter 122C - Mental Health, Developmental Disabilities, and Substance Abuse Act of 1985	67
Chapter 122C - Mental Health, Developmental Disabilities, and Substance Abuse Act of 1985 (Continuation)	68
Chapter 122D - North Carolina Agricultural Finance Act	68

Chapter 122E - North Carolina Housing Trust and Oil Overcharge Act	68
Chapter 123 - Impeachment	69
Chapter 123A - Industrial Development [Repealed.]	69
Chapter 124 - Internal Improvements	69
Chapter 125 - Libraries	69
Chapter 126 - State Personnel System	69
Chapter 127 - Militia [Repealed.]	69
Chapter 127A - Militia	69
Chapter 127B - Military Affairs	69
Chapter 127C - Advisory Commission on Military Affairs	69
Chapter 128 - Offices and Public Officers	69
Chapter 128 - Offices and Public Officers (Continuation)	70
Chapter 129 - Public Buildings and Grounds	70
Chapter 130 - Public Health [Repealed.]	70
Chapter 130A - Public Health	70
Chapter 130A - Public Health (Continuation)	71
Chapter 130A - Public Health (Continuation)	72
Chapter 130B - Hazardous Waste Management Commission [Repealed.]	72
Chapter 131 - Public Hospitals [Repealed.]	72
Chapter 131A - Health Care Facilities Finance Act	72
Chapter 131B - Licensing of Ambulatory Surgical Facilities [Repealed.]	72
Chapter 131C - Charitable Solicitation Licensure Act [Repealed.]	72
Chapter 131D - Inspection and Licensing of Facilities	72
Chapter 131E - Health Care Facilities and Services	72
Chapter 131E - Health Care Facilities and Services (Continuation)	73
Chapter 131F - Solicitation of Contributions	73
Chapter 132 - Public Records	73
Chapter 133 - Public Works	74
Chapter 134 - Youth Development [Recodified.]	74
Chapter 134A - Youth Services [Repealed.]	74
Chapter 135 - Retirement System for Teachers and State Employees; Social Security; Health Insurance Program for Children	74
Chapter 135 - Retirement System for Teachers and State Employees; Social Security; Health Insurance Program for Children	75
Chapter 136 - Transportation	75
Chapter 136 - Transportation (Continuation)	76
Chapter 137 - Rural Rehabilitation [Repealed.]	76
Chapter 138 - Salaries, Fees and Allowances	76
Chapter 138A - State Government Ethics Act	76
Chapter 139 - Soil and Water Conservation Districts	76

Chapter	Page
Chapter 140 - State Art Museum; Symphony and Art Societies	76
Chapter 140A - State Awards System	76
Chapter 141 - State Boundaries	76
Chapter 142 - State Debt	76
Chapter 143 - State Departments, Institutions, and Commissions	77
Chapter 143 - State Departments, Institutions, and Commissions (Continuation)	78
Chapter 143 - State Departments, Institutions, and Commissions (Continuation)	79
Chapter 143 - State Departments, Institutions, and Commissions (Continuation)	80
Chapter 143A - State Government Reorganization	80
Chapter 143B - Executive Organization Act of 1973	80
Chapter 143B - Executive Organization Act of 1973 (Continuation)	81
Chapter 143B - Executive Organization Act of 1973 (Continuation)	82
Chapter 143C - State Budget Act	83
Chapter 143D - The State Governmental Accountability and Internal Control Act	83
Chapter 144 - State Flag, Official Governmental Flags, Motto, and Colors	83
Chapter 145 - State Symbols and Other Official Adoptions.	83
Chapter 146 - State Lands	83
Chapter 147 - State Officers	83
Chapter 148 - State Prison System	84
Chapter 149 - State Song and Toast	84
Chapter 150 - Uniform Revocation of Licenses [Repealed.]	84
Chapter 150A - Administrative Procedure Act [Recodified.]	84
Chapter 150B - Administrative Procedure Act	84
Chapter 151 - Constables [Repealed.]	84
Chapter 152 - Coroners	84
Chapter 152A - County Medical Examiner [Repealed.]	84
Chapter 152A - County Medical Examiner [Repealed.] (Continuation)	85
Chapter 153 - Counties and County Commissioners [Repealed.]	85
Chapter 153A - Counties	85
Chapter 153B - Mountain Resources Planning Act	85
Chapter 153C - Uwharrie Regional Resources Act	85
Chapter 154 - County Surveyor [Repealed.]	85
Chapter 155 - County Treasurer [Repealed.]	85
Chapter 156 - Drainage	85
Chapter 156 – Drainage (Continuation)	86

Chapter 157 - Housing Authorities and Projects	86
Chapter 157A - Historic Properties Commissions [Transferred.]	86
Chapter 158 - Local Development	86
Chapter 159 - Local Government Finance	86
Chapter 159 - Local Government Finance (Continuation)	87
Chapter 159A - Pollution Abatement and Industrial Facilities Financing Act [Unconstitutional.]	87
Chapter 159B - Joint Municipal Electric Power and Energy Act	87
Chapter 159C - Industrial and Pollution Control Facilities Financing Act	87
Chapter 159D - The North Carolina Capital Facilities Financing Act	87
Chapter 159E - Registered Public Obligations Act	87
Chapter 159F - North Carolina Energy Development Authority [Repealed.]	87
Chapter 159G - Water Infrastructure	87
Chapter 159H - [Reserved.]	87
Chapter 159I - Solid Waste Management Loan Program and Local Government Special Obligation Bonds	87
Chapter 160 - Municipal Corporations [Repealed And Transferred.]	87
Chapter 160A - Cities and Towns	88
Chapter 160A - Cities and Towns (Continuation)	89
Chapter 160B - Consolidated City-County Act	89
Chapter 160C - Baseball Park Districts [Repealed.]	90
Chapter 161 - Register of Deeds	90
Chapter 162 - Sheriff	90
Chapter 162A - Water and Sewer Systems	90
Chapter 162B Continuity of Local Government in Emergency.	90
Chapter 163 Elections and Election Laws.	90
Chapter 163 Elections and Election Laws. (Continuation)	91
Chapter 164 Concerning the General Statutes of North Carolina.	92
Chapter 165 Veterans.	92
Chapter 166 Civil Preparedness Agencies [Repealed.]	92
Chapter 166A North Carolina Emergency Management Act.	92
Chapter 167 State Civil Air Patrol [Repealed.]	92
Chapter 168 Persons with Disabilities.	92
Chapter 168A Persons With Disabilities Protection Act.	92

Article 8.

Investment Securities.

(Revised)

Part 1.

Short Title and General Matters.

§ 25-8-101. Short title.

This Article may be cited as Uniform Commercial Code - Investment Securities. (1965, c. 700, s. 1; 1997-181, s. 1.)

§ 25-8-102. Definitions.

(a)   In this Article:

(1)   "Adverse claim" means a claim that a claimant has a property interest in a financial asset and that it is a violation of the rights of the claimant for another person to hold, transfer, or deal with the financial asset.

(2)   "Bearer form", as applied to a certificated security, means a form in which the security is payable to the bearer of the security certificate according to its terms but not by reason of an indorsement.

(3)   "Broker" means a person defined as a broker or dealer under the federal securities laws, but without excluding a bank acting in that capacity.

(4)   "Certificated security" means a security that is represented by a certificate.

(5)   "Clearing corporation" means:

(i)   A person that is registered as a "clearing agency" under the federal securities laws;

(ii)   A federal reserve bank; or

(iii) Any other person that provides clearance or settlement services with respect to financial assets that would require it to register as a clearing agency under the federal securities laws but for an exclusion or exemption from the registration requirement, if its activities as a clearing corporation, including promulgation of rules, are subject to regulation by a federal or state governmental authority.

(6) "Communicate" means to:

(i) Send a signed writing; or

(ii) Transmit information by any mechanism agreed upon by the persons transmitting and receiving the information.

(7) "Entitlement holder" means a person identified in the records of a securities intermediary as the person having a security entitlement against the securities intermediary. If a person acquires a security entitlement by virtue of G.S. 25-8-501(b)(2)or (3), that person is the entitlement holder.

(8) "Entitlement order" means a notification communicated to a securities intermediary directing transfer or redemption of a financial asset to which the entitlement holder has a security entitlement.

(9) "Financial asset", except as otherwise provided in G.S. 25-8-103, means:

(i) A security;

(ii) An obligation of a person or a share, participation, or other interest in a person or in property or an enterprise of a person, which is, or is of a type, dealt in or traded on financial markets, or which is recognized in any area in which it is issued or dealt in as a medium for investment; or

(iii) Any property that is held by a securities intermediary for another person in a securities account if the securities intermediary has expressly agreed with the other person that the property is to be treated as a financial asset under this Article.

As context requires, the term means either the interest itself or the means by which a person's claim to it is evidenced, including a certificated or uncertificated security, a security certificate, or a security entitlement.

(10) Repealed by Session Laws 2006-112, s. 20, effective October 1, 2006.

(11) "Indorsement" means a signature that alone or accompanied by other words is made on a security certificate in registered form or on a separate document for the purpose of assigning, transferring, or redeeming the security or granting a power to assign, transfer, or redeem it.

(12) "Instruction" means a notification communicated to the issuer of an uncertificated security which directs that the transfer of the security be registered or that the security be redeemed.

(13) "Registered form", as applied to a certificated security, means a form in which:

(i) The security certificate specifies a person entitled to the security; and

(ii) A transfer of the security may be registered upon books maintained for that purpose by or on behalf of the issuer, or the security certificate so states.

(14) "Securities intermediary" means:

(i) A clearing corporation; or

(ii) A person, including a bank or broker, that in the ordinary course of its business maintains securities accounts for others and is acting in that capacity.

(15) "Security", except as otherwise provided in G.S. 25-8-103, means an obligation of an issuer or a share, participation, or other interest in an issuer or in property or an enterprise of an issuer:

(i) Which is represented by a security certificate in bearer or registered form, or the transfer of which may be registered upon books maintained for that purpose by or on behalf of the issuer;

(ii) Which is one of a class or series or by its terms is divisible into a class or series of shares, participations, interests, or obligations; and

(iii) Which:

(A) Is, or is of a type, dealt in or traded on securities exchanges or securities markets; or

(B) Is a medium for investment and by its terms expressly provides that it is a security governed by this Article.

(16) "Security certificate" means a certificate representing a security.

(17) "Security entitlement" means the rights and property interest of an entitlement holder with respect to a financial asset specified in Part 5 of this Article.

(18) "Uncertificated security" means a security that is not represented by a certificate.

(b) Other definitions applying to this Article and the sections in which they appear are:

"Appropriate person"	G.S. 25-8-107.
"Control"	G.S. 25-8-106.
"Delivery"	G.S. 25-8-301.
"Investment company security"	G.S. 25-8-103.
"Issuer"	G.S. 25-8-201.
"Overissue"	G.S. 25-8-210.
"Protected purchaser"	G.S. 25-8-303.
"Securities account"	G.S. 25-8-501.

(c) In addition, Article 1 of this Chapter contains general definitions and principles of construction and interpretation applicable throughout this Article.

(d) The characterization of a person, business, or transaction for purposes of this Article does not determine the characterization of the person, business, or transaction for purposes of any other law, regulation, or rule. (1965, c. 700, s.

1; 1973, c. 497, s. 3; 1989, c. 588, s. 1; 1989 (Reg. Sess., 1990), c. 1024, s. 9(a); 1997-181, s. 1; 2006-112, s. 20.)

§ 25-8-103. Rules for determining whether certain obligations and interests are securities or financial assets.

(a)   A share or similar equity interest issued by a corporation, business trust, joint stock company, or similar entity is a security.

(b)   An "investment company security" is a security. "Investment company security" means a share or similar equity interest issued by an entity that is registered as an investment company under the federal investment company laws, an interest in a unit investment trust that is so registered, or a face-amount certificate issued by a face-amount certificate company that is so registered. Investment company security does not include an insurance policy or endowment policy or annuity contract issued by an insurance company.

(c)   An interest in a partnership or limited liability company is not a security unless it is dealt in or traded on securities exchanges or in securities markets, its terms expressly provide that it is a security governed by this Article, or it is an investment company security. However, an interest in a partnership or limited liability company is a financial asset if it is held in a securities account.

(d)   A writing that is a security certificate is governed by this Article and not by Article 3 of this Chapter, even though it also meets the requirements of that Article. However, a negotiable instrument governed by Article 3 is a financial asset if it is held in a securities account.

(e)   An option or similar obligation issued by a clearing corporation to its participants is not a security, but is a financial asset.

(f)   A commodity contract, as defined in G.S. 25-9-102(a)(15), is not a security or financial asset.

(g)   A document of title is not a financial asset unless G.S. 25-8-102(a)(9)(iii) applies. (1941, c. 353, s. 15; G.S., s. 55-95; 1955, c. 1371, s. 2; 1965, c. 700, s. 1; 1989, c. 588, s. 1; 1997-181, s. 1; 1998-217, s. 5; 2000-169, s. 21; 2006-112, s. 43.)

§ 25-8-104. Acquisition of security or financial asset or interest therein.

(a) A person acquires a security or an interest therein, under this Article, if:

(1) The person is a purchaser to whom a security is delivered pursuant to G.S. 25-8-301; or

(2) The person acquires a security entitlement to the security pursuant to G.S. 25-8-501.

(b) A person acquires a financial asset, other than a security, or an interest therein, under this Article, if the person acquires a security entitlement to the financial asset.

(c) A person who acquires a security entitlement to a security or other financial asset has the rights specified in Part 5 of this Article, but is a purchaser of any security, security entitlement, or other financial asset held by the securities intermediary only to the extent provided in G.S. 25-8-503.

(d) Unless the context shows that a different meaning is intended, a person who is required by other law, regulation, rule, or agreement to transfer, deliver, present, surrender, exchange, or otherwise put in the possession of another person a security or financial asset satisfies that requirement by causing the other person to acquire an interest in the security or financial asset pursuant to subsection (a) or (b) of this section. (1965, c. 700, s. 1; 1989, c. 588, s. 1; 1997-181, s. 1.)

§ 25-8-105. Notice of adverse claim.

(a) A person has notice of an adverse claim if:

(1) The person knows of the adverse claim;

(2) The person is aware of facts sufficient to indicate that there is a significant probability that the adverse claim exists and deliberately avoids information that would establish the existence of the adverse claim; or

(3)   The person has a duty, imposed by statute or regulation, to investigate whether an adverse claim exists, and the investigation so required would establish the existence of the adverse claim.

(b)   Having knowledge that a financial asset or interest therein is or has been transferred by a representative imposes no duty of inquiry into the rightfulness of a transaction and is not notice of an adverse claim. However, a person who knows that a representative has transferred a financial asset or interest therein in a transaction that is, or whose proceeds are being used, for the individual benefit of the representative or otherwise in breach of duty has notice of an adverse claim.

(c)   An act or event that creates a right to immediate performance of the principal obligation represented by a security certificate or sets a date on or after which the certificate is to be presented or surrendered for redemption or exchange does not itself constitute notice of an adverse claim except in the case of a transfer more than:

(1)   One year after a date set for presentment or surrender for redemption or exchange; or

(2)   Six months after a date set for payment of money against presentation or surrender of the certificate if money was available for payment on that date.

(d)   A purchaser of a certificated security has notice of an adverse claim if the security certificate:

(1)   Whether in bearer or registered form, has been indorsed "for collection" or "for surrender" or for some other purpose not involving transfer; or

(2)   Is in bearer form and has on it an unambiguous statement that it is the property of a person other than the transferor, but the mere writing of a name on the certificate is not such a statement.

(e)   Filing of a financing statement under Article 9 of this Chapter is not notice of an adverse claim to a financial asset. (1965, c. 700; s. 1; 1989, c. 588, s. 1; 1997-181, s. 1.)

§ 25-8-106. Control.

(a) A purchaser has "control" of a certificated security in bearer form if the certificated security is delivered to the purchaser.

(b) A purchaser has "control" of a certificated security in registered form if the certificated security is delivered to the purchaser, and:

(1) The certificate is endorsed to the purchaser or in blank by an effective endorsement; or

(2) The certificate is registered in the name of the purchaser, upon original issue or registration of transfer by the issuer.

(c) A purchaser has "control" of an uncertificated security if:

(1) The uncertificated security is delivered to the purchaser; or

(2) The issuer has agreed that it will comply with instructions originated by the purchaser without further consent by the registered owner.

(d) A purchaser has "control" of a security entitlement if:

(1) The purchaser becomes the entitlement holder;

(2) The securities intermediary has agreed that it will comply with entitlement orders originated by the purchaser without further consent by the entitlement holder; or

(3) Another person has control of the security entitlement on behalf of the purchaser or, having previously acquired control of the security entitlement, acknowledges that it has control on behalf of the purchaser.

(e) If an interest in a security entitlement is granted by the entitlement holder to the entitlement holder's own securities intermediary, the securities intermediary has control.

(f) A purchaser who has satisfied the requirements of subsection (c) or (d) of this section has control, even if the registered owner in the case of subsection (c) of this section or the entitlement holder in the case of subsection (d) of this section retains the right to make substitutions for the uncertificated security or security entitlement, to originate instructions or entitlement orders to the issuer or securities intermediary, or otherwise to deal with the uncertificated security or security entitlement.

(g) An issuer or a securities intermediary may not enter into an agreement of the kind described in subdivision (c)(2) or (d)(2) of this section without the consent of the registered owner or entitlement holder, but an issuer or a securities intermediary is not required to enter into such an agreement even though the registered owner or entitlement holder so directs. An issuer or securities intermediary that has entered into such an agreement is not required to confirm the existence of the agreement to another party unless requested to do so by the registered owner or entitlement holder. (1965, c. 700, s. 1; 1989, c. 588, s. 1; 1997-181, s. 1; 2000-169, s. 22.)

§ 25-8-107. Whether indorsement, instruction, or entitlement order is effective.

(a) "Appropriate person" means:

(1) With respect to an indorsement, the person specified by a security certificate or by an effective special indorsement to be entitled to the security;

(2) With respect to an instruction, the registered owner of an uncertificated security;

(3) With respect to an entitlement order, the entitlement holder;

(4) If the person designated in subdivision (1), (2), or (3) of this subsection is deceased, the designated person's successor taking under other law or the designated person's personal representative acting for the estate of the decedent; or

(5) If the person designated in subdivision (1), (2), or (3) of this subsection lacks capacity, the designated person's guardian, conservator, or other similar representative who has power under other law to transfer the security or financial asset.

(b) An indorsement, instruction, or entitlement order is effective if:

(1) It is made by the appropriate person;

(2) It is made by a person who has power under the law of agency to transfer the security or financial asset on behalf of the appropriate person, including, in the case of an instruction or entitlement order, a person who has control under G.S. 25-8-106(c)(2) or (d)(2); or

(3) The appropriate person has ratified it or is otherwise precluded from asserting its ineffectiveness.

(c) An indorsement, instruction, or entitlement order made by a representative is effective even if:

(1) The representative has failed to comply with a controlling instrument or with the law of the state having jurisdiction of the representative relationship, including any law requiring the representative to obtain court approval of the transaction; or

(2) The representative's action in making the indorsement, instruction, or entitlement order or using the proceeds of the transaction is otherwise a breach of duty.

(d) If a security is registered in the name of or specially indorsed to a person described as a representative, or if a securities account is maintained in the name of a person described as a representative, an indorsement, instruction, or entitlement order made by the person is effective even though the person is no longer serving in the described capacity.

(e) Effectiveness of an indorsement, instruction, or entitlement order is determined as of the date the indorsement, instruction, or entitlement order is made, and an indorsement, instruction, or entitlement order does not become ineffective by reason of any later change of circumstances. (1965, c. 700, s. 1; 1989, c. 588, s. 1; 1997-181, s. 1.)

§ 25-8-108. Warranties in direct holding.

(a) A person who transfers a certificated security to a purchaser for value warrants to the purchaser, and an indorser, if the transfer is by indorsement, warrants to any subsequent purchaser, that:

(1) The certificate is genuine and has not been materially altered;

(2) The transferor or indorser does not know of any fact that might impair the validity of the security;

(3) There is no adverse claim to the security;

(4) The transfer does not violate any restriction on transfer;

(5) If the transfer is by indorsement, the indorsement is made by an appropriate person, or if the indorsement is by an agent, the agent has actual authority to act on behalf of the appropriate person; and

(6) The transfer is otherwise effective and rightful.

(b) A person who originates an instruction for registration of transfer of an uncertificated security to a purchaser for value warrants to the purchaser that:

(1) The instruction is made by an appropriate person, or if the instruction is by an agent, the agent has actual authority to act on behalf of the appropriate person;

(2) The security is valid;

(3) There is no adverse claim to the security; and

(4) At the time the instruction is presented to the issuer:

(i) The purchaser will be entitled to the registration of transfer;

(ii) The transfer will be registered by the issuer free from all liens, security interests, restrictions, and claims other than those specified in the instruction;

(iii) The transfer will not violate any restriction on transfer; and

(iv) The requested transfer will otherwise be effective and rightful.

(c) A person who transfers an uncertificated security to a purchaser for value and does not originate an instruction in connection with the transfer warrants that:

(1) The uncertificated security is valid;

(2) There is no adverse claim to the security;

(3) The transfer does not violate any restriction on transfer; and

(4) The transfer is otherwise effective and rightful.

(d) A person who indorses a security certificate warrants to the issuer that:

(1) There is no adverse claim to the security; and

(2) The indorsement is effective.

(e) A person who originates an instruction for registration of transfer of an uncertificated security warrants to the issuer that:

(1) The instruction is effective; and

(2) At the time the instruction is presented to the issuer the purchaser will be entitled to the registration of transfer.

(f) A person who presents a certificated security for registration of transfer or for payment or exchange warrants to the issuer that the person is entitled to the registration, payment, or exchange, but a purchaser for value and without notice of adverse claims to whom transfer is registered warrants only that the person has no knowledge of any unauthorized signature in a necessary indorsement.

(g) If a person acts as agent of another in delivering a certificated security to a purchaser, the identity of the principal was known to the person to whom the certificate was delivered, and the certificate delivered by the agent was received by the agent from the principal or received by the agent from another person at the direction of the principal, the person delivering the security certificate warrants only that the delivering person has authority to act for the principal and does not know of any adverse claim to the certificated security.

(h) A secured party who redelivers a security certificate received, or after payment and on order of the debtor delivers the security certificate to another person, makes only the warranties of an agent under subsection (g) of this section.

(i) Except as otherwise provided in subsection (g) of this section, a broker acting for a customer makes to the issuer and a purchaser the warranties provided in subsections (a) through (f) of this section. A broker that delivers a security certificate to its customer, or causes its customer to be registered as the owner of an uncertificated security, makes to the customer the warranties provided in subsection (a) or (b) of this section, and has the rights and privileges of a purchaser under this section. The warranties of and in favor of the broker acting as an agent are in addition to applicable warranties given by and in favor of the customer. (1989, c. 588, s. 1; 1997-181, s. 1.)

§ 25-8-109. Warranties in indirect holding.

(a) A person who originates an entitlement order to a securities intermediary warrants to the securities intermediary that:

(1) The entitlement order is made by an appropriate person, or if the entitlement order is by an agent, the agent has actual authority to act on behalf of the appropriate person; and

(2) There is no adverse claim to the security entitlement.

(b) A person who delivers a security certificate to a securities intermediary for credit to a securities account or originates an instruction with respect to an uncertificated security directing that the uncertificated security be credited to a securities account makes to the securities intermediary the warranties specified in G.S. 25-8-108(a) or (b).

(c) If a securities intermediary delivers a security certificate to its entitlement holder or causes its entitlement holder to be registered as the owner of an uncertificated security, the securities intermediary makes to the entitlement holder the warranties specified in G.S. 25-8-108(a) or (b). (1997-181, s. 1.)

§ 25-8-110. Applicability; choice of law.

(a) The local law of the issuer's jurisdiction, as specified in subsection (d) of this section, governs:

(1) The validity of a security;

(2) The rights and duties of the issuer with respect to registration of transfer;

(3) The effectiveness of registration of transfer by the issuer;

(4) Whether the issuer owes any duties to an adverse claimant to a security; and

(5) Whether an adverse claim can be asserted against a person to whom transfer of a certificated or uncertificated security is registered or a person who obtains control of an uncertificated security.

(b) The local law of the securities intermediary's jurisdiction, as specified in subsection (e) of this section, governs:

(1) Acquisition of a security entitlement from the securities intermediary;

(2) The rights and duties of the securities intermediary and entitlement holder arising out of a security entitlement;

(3) Whether the securities intermediary owes any duties to an adverse claimant to a security entitlement; and

(4) Whether an adverse claim can be asserted against a person who acquires a security entitlement from the securities intermediary or a person who purchases a security entitlement or interest therein from an entitlement holder.

(c) The local law of the jurisdiction in which a security certificate is located at the time of delivery governs whether an adverse claim can be asserted against a person to whom the security certificate is delivered.

(d) "Issuer's jurisdiction" means the jurisdiction under which the issuer of the security is organized or, if permitted by the law of that jurisdiction, the law of another jurisdiction specified by the issuer. An issuer organized under the law of this State may specify the law of another jurisdiction as the law governing the matters specified in subdivisions (a)(2) through (5) of this section.

(e) The following rules determine a "securities intermediary's jurisdiction" for purposes of this section:

(1)   If an agreement between the securities intermediary and its entitlement holder governing the securities account expressly provides that a particular jurisdiction is the securities intermediary's jurisdiction for purposes of this Part, this Article, or this Chapter, that jurisdiction is the securities intermediary's jurisdiction.

(2)   If subdivision (1) of this subsection does not apply and an agreement between the securities intermediary and its entitlement holder governing the securities account expressly provides that the agreement is governed by the law of a particular jurisdiction, that jurisdiction is the securities intermediary's jurisdiction.

(3)   If neither subdivision (1) nor subdivision (2) of this section applies and an agreement between the securities intermediary and its entitlement holder governing the securities account expressly provides that the securities account is maintained at an office in a particular jurisdiction, that jurisdiction is the securities intermediary's jurisdiction.

(4)   If none of the preceding subdivisions applies, the securities intermediary's jurisdiction is the jurisdiction in which the office identified in an account statement as the office serving the entitlement holder's account is located.

(5)   If none of the preceding subdivisions applies, the securities intermediary's jurisdiction is the jurisdiction in which the chief executive office of the securities intermediary is located.

(f)   A securities intermediary's jurisdiction is not determined by the physical location of certificates representing financial assets, or by the jurisdiction in which is organized the issuer of the financial asset with respect to which an entitlement holder has a security entitlement, or by the location of facilities for data processing or other record keeping concerning the account. (1997-181, s. 1; 2000-169, s. 23.)

§ 25-8-111. Clearing corporation rules.

A rule adopted by a clearing corporation governing rights and obligations among the clearing corporation and its participants in the clearing corporation is effective even if the rule conflicts with this Article and affects another party who does not consent to the rule. (1997-181, s. 1.)

§ 25-8-112. Creditor's legal process.

(a)   The interest of a debtor in a certificated security may be reached by a creditor only by actual seizure of the security certificate by the officer making the attachment or levy, except as otherwise provided in subsection (d) of this section. However, a certificated security for which the certificate has been surrendered to the issuer may be reached by a creditor by legal process upon the issuer.

(b)   The interest of a debtor in an uncertificated security may be reached by a creditor only by legal process upon the issuer at its chief executive office in the United States, except as otherwise provided in subsection (d) of this section.

(c)   The interest of a debtor in a security entitlement may be reached by a creditor only by legal process upon the securities intermediary with whom the debtor's securities account is maintained, except as otherwise provided in subsection (d) of this section.

(d)   The interest of a debtor in a certificated security for which the certificate is in the possession of a secured party, or in an uncertificated security registered in the name of a secured party, or a security entitlement maintained in the name of a secured party, may be reached by a creditor by legal process upon the secured party.

(e)   A creditor whose debtor is the owner of a certificated security, uncertificated security, or security entitlement is entitled to aid from a court of competent jurisdiction, by injunction or otherwise, in reaching the certificated security, uncertificated security, or security entitlement or in satisfying the claim by means allowed at law or in equity in regard to property that cannot readily be reached by other legal process. (1997-181, s. 1.)

§ 25-8-113. Statute of frauds inapplicable.

A contract or modification of a contract for the sale or purchase of a security is enforceable whether or not there is a writing signed or record authenticated by a party against whom enforcement is sought, even if the contract or modification is not capable of performance within one year of its making. (1997-181, s. 1.)

§ 25-8-114. Evidentiary rules concerning certificated securities.

The following rules apply in an action on a certificated security against the issuer:

(1)   Unless specifically denied in the pleadings, each signature on a security certificate or in a necessary indorsement is admitted.

(2)   If the effectiveness of a signature is put in issue, the burden of establishing effectiveness is on the party claiming under the signature, but the signature is presumed to be genuine or authorized.

(3)   If signatures on a security certificate are admitted or established, production of the certificate entitles a holder to recover on it unless the defendant establishes a defense or a defect going to the validity of the security.

(4)   If it is shown that a defense or defect exists, the plaintiff has the burden of establishing that the plaintiff or some person under whom the plaintiff claims is a person against whom the defense or defect cannot be asserted. (1997-181, s. 1.)

§ 25-8-115. Securities intermediary and others not liable to adverse claimant.

A securities intermediary that has transferred a financial asset pursuant to an effective entitlement order, or a broker or other agent or bailee that has dealt with a financial asset at the direction of its customer or principal, is not liable to a person having an adverse claim to the financial asset, unless the securities intermediary, or broker or other agent or bailee:

(1)   Took the action after it had been served with an injunction, restraining order, or other legal process enjoining it from doing so, issued by a court of

competent jurisdiction, and had a reasonable opportunity to act on the injunction, restraining order, or other legal process; or

(2) Acted in collusion with the wrongdoer in violating the rights of the adverse claimant; or

(3) In the case of a security certificate that has been stolen, acted with notice of the adverse claim. (1997-181, s. 1.)

§ 25-8-116. Securities intermediary as purchaser for value.

A securities intermediary that receives a financial asset and establishes a security entitlement to the financial asset in favor of an entitlement holder is a purchaser for value of the financial asset. A securities intermediary that acquires a security entitlement to a financial asset from another securities intermediary acquires the security entitlement for value if the securities intermediary acquiring the security entitlement establishes a security entitlement to the financial asset in favor of an entitlement holder. (1997-181, s. 1.)

Part 2.

Issue and Issuer.

§ 25-8-201. Issuer.

(a) With respect to an obligation on or a defense to a security, an "issuer" includes a person that:

(1) Places or authorizes the placing of its name on a security certificate, other than as authenticating trustee, registrar, transfer agent, or the like, to evidence a share, participation, or other interest in its property or in an enterprise, or to evidence its duty to perform an obligation represented by the certificate;

(2) Creates a share, participation, or other interest in its property or in an enterprise, or undertakes an obligation, that is an uncertificated security;

(3) Directly or indirectly creates a fractional interest in its rights or property, if the fractional interest is represented by a security certificate; or

(4) Becomes responsible for, or in place of, another person described as an issuer in this section.

(b) With respect to an obligation on or defense to a security, a guarantor is an issuer to the extent of its guaranty, whether or not its obligation is noted on a security certificate.

(c) With respect to a registration of a transfer, issuer means a person on whose behalf transfer books are maintained. (1899, c. 733, ss. 29, 60 to 62; Rev., ss. 2177, 2209 to 2211; C.S., ss. 3009, 3041 to 3043; 1965, c. 700, s. 1; 1989, c. 588, s. 1; 1989 (Reg. Sess., 1990), c. 1024, s. 9(b); 1997-181, s. 1.)

§ 25-8-202. Issuer's responsibility and defenses; notice of defect or defense.

(a) Even against a purchaser for value and without notice, the terms of a certificated security include terms stated on the certificate and terms made part of the security by reference on the certificate to another instrument, indenture, or document or to a constitution, statute, ordinance, rule, regulation, order, or the like, to the extent the terms referred to do not conflict with terms stated on the certificate. A reference under this subsection does not of itself charge a purchaser for value with notice of a defect going to the validity of the security, even if the certificate expressly states that a person accepting it admits notice. The terms of an uncertificated security include those stated in any instrument, indenture, or document or in a constitution, statute, ordinance, rule, regulation, order, or the like, pursuant to which the security is issued.

(b) The following rules apply if an issuer asserts that a security is not valid:

(1) A security other than one issued by a government or governmental subdivision, agency, or instrumentality, even though issued with a defect going to its validity, is valid in the hands of a purchaser for value and without notice of the particular defect unless the defect involves a violation of a constitutional provision. In that case, the security is valid in the hands of a purchaser for value and without notice of the defect, other than one who takes by original issue.

(2) Subdivision (1) of this subsection applies to an issuer that is a government or governmental subdivision, agency, or instrumentality only if there has been substantial compliance with the legal requirements governing the issue or the issuer has received a substantial consideration for the issue as a whole or for the particular security and a stated purpose of the issue is one for which the issuer has power to borrow money or issue the security.

(c) Except as otherwise provided in G.S. 25-8-205, lack of genuineness of a certificated security is a complete defense, even against a purchaser for value and without notice.

(d) All other defenses of the issuer of a security, including nondelivery and conditional delivery of a certificated security, are ineffective against a purchaser for value who has taken the security without notice of the particular defense.

(e) This section does not affect the right of a party to cancel a contract for a security "when, as and if issued" or "when distributed" in the event of a material change in the character of the security that is the subject of the contract or in the plan or arrangement pursuant to which the security is to be issued or distributed.

(f) If a security is held by a securities intermediary against whom an entitlement holder has a security entitlement with respect to the security, the issuer may not assert any defense that the issuer could not assert if the entitlement holder held the security directly. (1899, c. 733, ss. 23, 28, 56, 57, 61, 62; Rev., ss. 2171, 2176, 2205, 2206, 2210, 2211; C.S., ss. 3003, 3008, 3037, 3038, 3042, 3043; 1965, c. 700, s. 1; 1989, c. 588, s. 1; 1997-181, s. 1.)

§ 25-8-203. Staleness as notice of defect or defense.

After an act or event, other than a call that has been revoked, creating a right to immediate performance of the principal obligation represented by a certificated security or setting a date on or after which the security is to be presented or surrendered for redemption or exchange, a purchaser is charged with notice of any defect in its issue or defense of the issuer, if the act or event:

(1) Requires the payment of money, the delivery of a certificated security, the registration of transfer of an uncertificated security, or any of them on presentation or surrender of the security certificate, the money or security is

available on the date set for payment or exchange, and the purchaser takes the security more than one year after that date; or

(2) Is not covered by subdivision (1) of this section and the purchaser takes the security more than two years after the date set for surrender or presentation or the date on which performance became due. (1899, c. 733, ss. 52, 53; Rev., ss. 2201, 2202; C.S., ss. 3033, 3034; 1965, c. 700, s. 1; 1989, c. 588, s. 1; 1997-181, s. 1.)

§ 25-8-204. Effect of issuer's restriction on transfer.

A restriction on transfer of a security imposed by the issuer, even if otherwise lawful, is ineffective against a person without knowledge of the restriction unless:

(1) The security is certificated and the restriction is noted conspicuously on the security certificate; or

(2) The security is uncertificated and the registered owner has been notified of the restriction. (1941, c. 353, s. 15; G.S., s. 55-95; 1955, c. 1371, s. 2; 1965, c. 700, s. 1; 1989, c. 588, s. 1; 1997-181, s. 1.)

§ 25-8-205. Effect of unauthorized signature on security certificate.

An unauthorized signature placed on a security certificate before or in the course of issue is ineffective, but the signature is effective in favor of a purchaser for value of the certificated security if the purchaser is without notice of the lack of authority and the signing has been done by:

(1) An authenticating trustee, registrar, transfer agent, or other person entrusted by the issuer with the signing of the security certificate or of similar security certificates, or the immediate preparation for signing of any of them; or

(2) An employee of the issuer, or of any of the persons listed in subdivision (1) of this section, entrusted with responsible handling of the security certificate. (1899, c. 733, s. 23; Rev., s. 2171; C.S., s. 3003; 1965, c. 700, s. 1; 1989, c. 588, s. 1; 1997-181, s. 1.)

§ 25-8-206. Completion of alteration of security certificate.

(a)   If a security certificate contains the signatures necessary to its issue or transfer but is incomplete in any other respect:

(1)   Any person may complete it by filling in the blanks as authorized; and

(2)   Even if the blanks are incorrectly filled in, the security certificate as completed is enforceable by a purchaser who took it for value and without notice of the incorrectness.

(b)   A complete security certificate that has been improperly altered, even if fraudulently, remains enforceable, but only according to its original terms. (1899, c. 733, ss. 14, 15, 124; Rev., ss. 2164, 2165, 2274; C.S., ss. 2995, 2996, 3106; 1941, c. 353, s. 16; G.S., s. 55-96; 1955, c. 1371, s. 2; 1965, c. 700, s. 1; 1989, c. 588, s. 1; 1997-181, s. 1.)

§ 25-8-207. Rights and duties of issuer with respect to registered owners.

(a)   Before due presentment for registration of transfer of a certificated security in registered form or of an instruction requesting registration of transfer of an uncertificated security, the issuer or indenture trustee may treat the registered owner as the person exclusively entitled to vote, receive notifications, and otherwise exercise all the rights and powers of an owner.

(b)   This Article does not affect the liability of the registered owner of a security for a call, assessment, or the like. (1941, c. 353, s. 3; G.S., s. 55-83; 1955, c. 1371, s. 2; 1965, c. 700, s. 1; 1989, c. 588, s. 1; 1997-181, s. 1.)

§ 25-8-208. Effect of signature of authenticating trustee, registrar, or transfer agent.

(a) A person signing a security certificate as authenticating trustee, registrar, transfer agent, or the like, warrants to a purchaser for value of the certificated security, if the purchaser is without notice of a particular defect, that:

(1) The certificate is genuine;

(2) The person's own participation in the issue of the security is within the person's capacity and within the scope of the authority received by the person from the issuer; and

(3) The person has reasonable grounds to believe that the certificated security is in the form and within the amount the issuer is authorized to issue.

(b) Unless otherwise agreed, a person signing under subsection (a) of this section does not assume responsibility for the validity of the security in other respects. (1965, c. 700, s. 1; 1989, c. 588, s. 1; 1997-181, s. 1.)

§ 25-8-209. Issuer's lien.

A lien in favor of an issuer upon a certificated security is valid against a purchaser only if the right of the issuer to the lien is noted conspicuously on the security certificate. (1997-181, s. 1.)

§ 25-8-210. Overissue.

(a) In this section, "overissue" means the issue of securities in excess of the amount the issuer has corporate power to issue, but an overissue does not occur if appropriate action has cured the overissue.

(b) Except as otherwise provided in subsections (c) and (d) of this section, the provisions of this Article which validate a security or compel its issue or reissue do not apply to the extent that validation, issue, or reissue would result in overissue.

(c) If an identical security not constituting an overissue is reasonably available for purchase, a person entitled to issue or validation may compel the issuer to purchase the security and deliver it if certificated or register its transfer if uncertificated, against surrender of any security certificate the person holds.

(d)   If a security is not reasonably available for purchase, a person entitled to issue or validation may recover from the issuer the price the person or the last purchaser for value paid for it with interest from the date of the person's demand. (1997-181, s. 1.)

Part 3.

Transfer of Certificated and Uncertificated Securities.

§ 25-8-301. Delivery.

(a)   Delivery of a certificated security to a purchaser occurs when:

(1)   The purchaser acquires possession of the security certificate;

(2)   Another person, other than a securities intermediary, either acquires possession of the security certificate on behalf of the purchaser or, having previously acquired possession of the certificate, acknowledges that it holds for the purchaser; or

(3)   A securities intermediary acting on behalf of the purchaser acquires possession of the security certificate, only if the certificate is in registered form and is (i) registered in the name of the purchaser, (ii) payable to the order of the purchaser, or (iii) specially indorsed to the purchaser by an effective indorsement and has not been indorsed to the securities intermediary or in blank.

(b)   Delivery of an uncertificated security to a purchaser occurs when:

(1)   The issuer registers the purchaser as the registered owner, upon original issue or registration of transfer; or

(2)   Another person, other than a securities intermediary, either becomes the registered owner of the uncertificated security on behalf of the purchaser or, having previously become the registered owner, acknowledges that it holds for the purchaser. (1899, c. 733, ss. 52, 57 to 59; Rev., ss. 2201, 2206 to 2208;

C.S., ss. 3033, 3038 to 3040; 1941, c. 353, ss. 6, 7; G.S., ss. 55-86, 55-87; 1955, c. 1371, s. 2; 1965, c. 700, s. 1; 1989, c. 588, s. 1; 1997-181, s. 1; 2000-169, s. 24.)

§ 25-8-302. Rights of purchaser.

(a) Except as otherwise provided in subsections (b) and (c) of this section, a purchaser of a certificated or uncertificated security acquires all rights in the security that the transferor had or had power to transfer.

(b) A purchaser of a limited interest acquires rights only to the extent of the interest purchased.

(c) A purchaser of a certificated security who as a previous holder had notice of an adverse claim does not improve its position by taking from a protected purchaser. (1899, c. 733, s. 52; Rev., s. 2201; C.S., s. 3033; 1965, c. 700, s. 1; 1989, c. 588, s. 1; 1997-181, s. 1; 2000-169, s. 25.)

§ 25-8-303. Protected purchaser.

(a) "Protected purchaser" means a purchaser of a certificated or uncertificated security, or of an interest therein, who:

(1) Gives value;

(2) Does not have notice of any adverse claim to the security; and

(3) Obtains control of the certificated or uncertificated security.

(b) In addition to acquiring the rights of a purchaser, a protected purchaser also acquires its interest in the security free of any adverse claim. (1965, c. 700, s. 1; 1997-181, s. 1.)

§ 25-8-304. Indorsement.

(a) An indorsement may be in blank or special. An indorsement in blank includes an indorsement to bearer. A special indorsement specifies to whom a security is to be transferred or who has power to transfer it. A holder may convert a blank indorsement to a special indorsement.

(b) An indorsement purporting to be only part of a security certificate representing units intended by the issuer to be separately transferable is effective to the extent of the indorsement.

(c) An indorsement, whether special or in blank, does not constitute a transfer until delivery of the certificate on which it appears or, if the indorsement is on a separate document, until delivery of both the document and the certificate.

(d) If a security certificate in registered form has been delivered to a purchaser without a necessary indorsement, the purchaser may become a protected purchaser only when the indorsement is supplied. However, against a transferor, a transfer is complete upon delivery and the purchaser has a specifically enforceable right to have any necessary indorsement supplied.

(e) An indorsement of a security certificate in bearer form may give notice of an adverse claim to the certificate, but it does not otherwise affect a right to registration that the holder possesses.

(f) Unless otherwise agreed, a person making an indorsement assumes only the obligations provided in G.S. 25-8-108 and not an obligation that the security will be honored by the issuer. (1899, c. 733, ss. 37, 56; Rev., ss. 2186, 2205; C.S., ss. 3018, 3037; 1965, c. 700, s. 1; 1989, c. 588, s. 1; 1997-181, s. 1.)

§ 25-8-305. Instruction.

(a) If an instruction has been originated by an appropriate person but is incomplete in any other respect, any person may complete it as authorized and the issuer may rely on it as completed, even though it has been completed incorrectly.

(b) Unless otherwise agreed, a person initiating an instruction assumes only the obligations imposed by G.S. 25-8-108 and not an obligation that the security will be honored by the issuer. (1899, c. 733, ss. 52, 53; Rev., ss. 2201, 2202; C.S., ss. 3033, 3034; 1965, c. 700, s. 1; 1989, c. 588, s. 1; 1997-181, s. 1.)

§ 25-8-306. Effect of guaranteeing signature, indorsement, or instruction.

(a)   A person who guarantees a signature of an indorser of a security certificate warrants that at the time of signing:

(1)   The signature was genuine;

(2)   The signer was an appropriate person to indorse, or if the signature is by an agent, the agent had actual authority to act on behalf of the appropriate person; and

(3)   The signer had legal capacity to sign.

(b)   A person who guarantees a signature of the originator of an instruction warrants that at the time of signing:

(1)   The signature was genuine;

(2)   The signer was an appropriate person to originate the instruction, or if the signature is by an agent, the agent had actual authority to act on behalf of the appropriate person, if the person specified in the instruction as the registered owner was, in fact, the registered owner, as to which fact the signature guarantor does not make a warranty; and

(3)   The signer had legal capacity to sign.

(c)   A person who specially guarantees the signature of an originator of an instruction makes the warranties of a signature guarantor under subsection (b) of this section and also warrants that at the time the instruction is presented to the issuer:

(1)   The person specified in the instruction as the registered owner of the uncertificated security will be the registered owner; and

(2) The transfer of the uncertificated security requested in the instruction will be registered by the issuer free from all liens, security interests, restrictions, and claims other than those specified in the instruction.

(d) A guarantor under subsections (a) and (b) of this section or a special guarantor under subsection (c) of this section does not otherwise warrant the rightfulness of the transfer.

(e) A person who guarantees an indorsement of a security certificate makes the warranties of a signature guarantor under subsection (a) of this section and also warrants the rightfulness of the transfer in all respects.

(f) A person who guarantees an instruction requesting the transfer of an uncertificated security makes the warranties of a special signature guarantor under subsection (c) of this section and also warrants the rightfulness of the transfer in all respects.

(g) An issuer may not require a special guaranty of signature, a guaranty of indorsement, or a guaranty of instruction as a condition to registration of transfer.

(h) The warranties under this section are made to a person taking or dealing with the security in reliance on the guaranty, and the guarantor is liable to the person for loss resulting from their breach. An indorser or originator of an instruction whose signature, indorsement, or instruction has been guaranteed is liable to a guarantor for any loss suffered by the guarantor as a result of breach of the warranties of the guarantor. (1899, c. 733, ss. 65 to 67, 69; Rev., ss. 2214 to 2216, 2218; C.S., ss. 3046 to 3048, 3050; 1941, c. 353, ss. 11, 12; G.S., ss. 55-91, 55-92; 1955, c. 1371, s. 2; 1965, c. 700, s. 1; 1989, c. 588, s. 1; 1997-181, s. 1.)

§ 25-8-307. Purchaser's right to requisites for registration of transfer.

Unless otherwise agreed, the transferor of a security on due demand shall supply the purchaser with proof of authority to transfer or with any other requisite necessary to obtain registration of the transfer of the security, but if the transfer is not for value, a transferor need not comply unless the purchaser pays the necessary expenses. If the transferor fails within a reasonable time to comply with the demand, the purchaser may reject or rescind the transfer.

(1899, c. 733, s. 49; Rev., s. 2198; C.S., s. 3030; 1941, c. 353, s. 9; G.S., s. 55-89; 1955, c. 1371, s. 2; 1965, c. 700, s. 1; 1989, c. 588, s. 1; 1997-181, s. 1.)

Part 4.

Registration.

§ 25-8-401. Duty of issuer to register transfer.

(a) If a certificated security in registered form is presented to an issuer with a request to register transfer or an instruction is presented to an issuer with a request to register transfer of an uncertificated security, the issuer shall register the transfer as requested if:

(1) Under the terms of the security the person seeking registration of transfer is eligible to have the security registered in its name;

(2) The indorsement or instruction is made by the appropriate person or by an agent who has actual authority to act on behalf of the appropriate person;

(3) Reasonable assurance is given that the indorsement or instruction is genuine and authorized (G.S. 25-8-402);

(4) Any applicable law relating to the collection of taxes has been complied with;

(5) The transfer does not violate any restriction on transfer imposed by the issuer in accordance with G.S. 25-8-204;

(6) A demand that the issuer not register transfer has not become effective under G.S. 25-8-403, or the issuer has complied with G.S. 25-8-403(b) but no legal process or indemnity bond is obtained as provided in G.S. 25-8-403(d); and

(7) The transfer is in fact rightful or is to a protected purchaser.

(b) If an issuer is under a duty to register a transfer of a security, the issuer is liable to a person presenting a certificated security or an instruction for registration or to the person's principal for loss resulting from unreasonable delay in registration or failure or refusal to register the transfer. (1965, c. 700, s. 1; 1989, c. 588, s. 1; 1997-181, s. 1.)

§ 25-8-402. Assurance that indorsement or instruction is effective.

(a) An issuer may require the following assurance that each necessary indorsement or each instruction is genuine and authorized:

(1) In all cases, a guaranty of the signature of the person making an indorsement or originating an instruction including, in the case of an instruction, reasonable assurance of identity;

(2) If the indorsement is made or the instruction is originated by an agent, appropriate assurance of actual authority to sign;

(3) If the indorsement is made or the instruction is originated by a fiduciary pursuant to G.S. 25-8-107(a)(4) or G.S. 25-8-107(a)(5), appropriate evidence of appointment or incumbency;

(4) If there is more than one fiduciary, reasonable assurance that all who are required to sign have done so; and

(5) If the indorsement is made or the instruction is originated by a person not covered by another provision of this subsection, assurance appropriate to the case corresponding as nearly as may be to the provisions of this subsection.

(b) An issuer may elect to require reasonable assurance beyond that specified in this section.

(c) In this section:

(1) "Guaranty of the signature" means a guaranty signed by or on behalf of a person reasonably believed by the issuer to be responsible. An issuer may adopt standards with respect to responsibility if they are not manifestly unreasonable.

(2) "Appropriate evidence of appointment or incumbency" means:

(i) In the case of a fiduciary appointed or qualified by a court, a certificate issued by or under the direction or supervision of the court or an officer thereof and dated within 60 days before the date of presentation for transfer; or

(ii) In any other case, a copy of a document showing the appointment or a certificate issued by or on behalf of a person reasonably believed by an issuer to be responsible or, in the absence of that document or certificate, other evidence the issuer reasonably considers appropriate. (1965, c. 700, s. 1; 1989, c. 588, s. 1; 1997-181, s. 1.)

§ 25-8-403. Demand that issuer not register transfer.

(a) A person who is an appropriate person to make an indorsement or originate an instruction may demand that the issuer not register transfer of a security by communicating to the issuer a notification that identifies the registered owner and the issue of which the security is a part and provides an address for communications directed to the person making the demand. The demand is effective only if it is received by the issuer at a time and in a manner affording the issuer reasonable opportunity to act on it.

(b) If a certificated security in registered form is presented to an issuer with a request to register transfer or an instruction is presented to an issuer with a request to register transfer of an uncertificated security after a demand that the issuer not register transfer has become effective, the issuer shall promptly communicate to (i) the person who initiated the demand at the address provided in the demand and (ii) the person who presented the security for registration of transfer or initiated the instruction requesting registration of transfer a notification stating that:

(1) The certificated security has been presented for registration of transfer or the instruction for registration of transfer of the uncertificated security has been received;

(2) A demand that the issuer not register transfer had previously been received; and

(3) The issuer will withhold registration of transfer for a period of time stated in the notification in order to provide the person who initiated the demand an opportunity to obtain legal process or an indemnity bond.

(c) The period described in subdivision (b)(3) of this section may not exceed 30 days after the date of communication of the notification. A shorter period may be specified by the issuer if it is not manifestly unreasonable.

(d) An issuer is not liable to a person who initiated a demand that the issuer not register transfer for any loss the person suffers as a result of registration of a transfer pursuant to an effective indorsement or instruction if the person who initiated the demand does not, within the time stated in the issuer's communication, either:

(1) Obtain an appropriate restraining order, injunction, or other process from a court of competent jurisdiction enjoining the issuer from registering the transfer; or

(2) File with the issuer an indemnity bond, sufficient in the issuer's judgment to protect the issuer and any transfer agent, registrar, or other agent of the issuer involved from any loss it or they may suffer by refusing to register the transfer.

(e) This section does not relieve an issuer from liability for registering transfer pursuant to an indorsement or instruction that was not effective. (1965, c. 700, s. 1; 1977, c. 814, s. 9; 1989, c. 588, s. 1; 1989 (Reg. Sess., 1990), c. 1024, s. 9(d); 1997-181, s. 1.)

§ 25-8-404. Wrongful registration.

(a) Except as otherwise provided in G.S. 25-8-406, an issuer is liable for wrongful registration of transfer if the issuer has registered a transfer of a security to a person not entitled to it, and the transfer was registered:

(1) Pursuant to an ineffective indorsement or instruction;

(2) After a demand that the issuer not register transfer became effective under G.S. 25-8-403(a) and the issuer did not comply with G.S. 25-8-403(b);

(3) After the issuer had been served with an injunction, restraining order, or other legal process enjoining it from registering the transfer, issued by a court of

competent jurisdiction, and the issuer had a reasonable opportunity to act on the injunction, restraining order, or other legal process; or

(4) By an issuer acting in collusion with the wrongdoer.

(b) An issuer that is liable for wrongful registration of transfer under subsection (a) of this section on demand shall provide the person entitled to the security with a like certificated or uncertificated security, and any payments or distributions that the person did not receive as a result of the wrongful registration. If an overissue would result, the issuer's liability to provide the person with a like security is governed by G.S. 25-8-210.

(c) Except as otherwise provided in subsection (a) of this section or in a law relating to the collection of taxes, an issuer is not liable to an owner or other person suffering loss as a result of the registration of a transfer of a security if registration was made pursuant to an effective indorsement or instruction. (1965, c. 700, s. 1; 1989, c. 588, s. 1; 1997-181, s. 1.)

§ 25-8-405. Replacement of lost, destroyed, or wrongfully taken security certificate.

(a) If an owner of a certificated security, whether in registered or bearer form, claims that the certificate has been lost, destroyed, or wrongfully taken, the issuer shall issue a new certificate if the owner:

(1) So requests before the issuer has notice that the certificate has been acquired by a protected purchaser;

(2) Files with the issuer a sufficient indemnity bond; and

(3) Satisfies other reasonable requirements imposed by the issuer.

(b) If, after the issue of a new security certificate, a protected purchaser of the original certificate presents it for registration of transfer, the issuer shall register the transfer unless an overissue would result. In that case, the issuer's liability is governed by G.S. 25-8-210. In addition to any rights on the indemnity bond, an issuer may recover the new certificate from a person to whom it was issued or any person taking under that person, except a protected purchaser.

(1941, c. 353, s. 20; G.S., s. 55-100; 1955, c. 1371, s. 2; 1965, c. 700, s. 1; 1989, c. 588, s. 1; 1997-181, s. 1.)

§ 25-8-406. Obligation to notify issuer of lost, destroyed, or wrongfully taken security certificate.

If a security certificate has been lost, apparently destroyed, or wrongfully taken, and the owner fails to notify the issuer of that fact within a reasonable time after the owner has notice of it and the issuer registers a transfer of the security before receiving notification, the owner may not assert against the issuer a claim for registering the transfer under G.S. 25-8-404 or a claim to a new security certificate under G.S. 25-8-405. (1965, c. 700, s. 1; 1989, c. 588, s. 1; 1997-181, s. 1.)

§ 25-8-407. Authenticating trustee, transfer agent, and registrar.

A person acting as authenticating trustee, transfer agent, registrar, or other agent for an issuer in the registration of a transfer of its securities, in the issue of new security certificates or uncertificated securities, or in the cancellation of surrendered security certificates has the same obligation to the holder or owner of a certificated or uncertificated security with regard to the particular functions performed as the issuer has in regard to those functions. (1989, c. 588, s. 1; 1997-181, s. 1.)

Part 5.

Security Entitlements.

§ 25-8-501. Securities account; acquisition of security entitlement from securities intermediary.

(a) "Securities account" means an account to which a financial asset is or may be credited in accordance with an agreement under which the person maintaining the account undertakes to treat the person for whom the account is maintained as entitled to exercise the rights that comprise the financial asset.

(b) Except as otherwise provided in subsections (d) and (e) of this section, a person acquires a security entitlement if a securities intermediary:

(1) Indicates by book entry that a financial asset has been credited to the person's securities account;

(2) Receives a financial asset from the person or acquires a financial asset for the person and, in either case, accepts it for credit to the person's securities account; or

(3) Becomes obligated under other law, regulation, or rule to credit a financial asset to the person's securities account.

(c) If a condition of subsection (b) of this section has been met, a person has a security entitlement even though the securities intermediary does not itself hold the financial asset.

(d) If a securities intermediary holds a financial asset for another person, and the financial asset is registered in the name of, payable to the order of, or specially indorsed to the other person, and has not been indorsed to the securities intermediary or in blank, the other person is treated as holding the financial asset directly rather than as having a security entitlement with respect to the financial asset.

(e) Issuance of a security is not establishment of a security entitlement. (1997-181, s. 1.)

§ 25-8-502. Assertion of adverse claim against entitlement holder.

An action based on an adverse claim to a financial asset, whether framed in conversion, replevin, constructive trust, equitable lien, or other theory, may not be asserted against a person who acquires a security entitlement under G.S. 25-8-501 for value and without notice of the adverse claim. (1997-181, s. 1.)

§ 25-8-503. Property interest of entitlement holder in financial asset held by securities intermediary.

(a) To the extent necessary for a securities intermediary to satisfy all security entitlements with respect to a particular financial asset, all interests in that financial asset held by the securities intermediary are held by the securities intermediary for the entitlement holders, are not property of the securities intermediary, and are not subject to claims of creditors of the securities intermediary, except as otherwise provided in G.S. 25-8-511.

(b) An entitlement holder's property interest with respect to a particular financial asset under subsection (a) of this section is a pro rata property interest in all interests in that financial asset held by the securities intermediary, without regard to the time the entitlement holder acquired the security entitlement or the time the securities intermediary acquired the interest in that financial asset.

(c) An entitlement holder's property interest with respect to a particular financial asset under subsection (a) of this section may be enforced against the securities intermediary only by exercise of the entitlement holder's rights under G.S. 25-8-505 through G.S. 25-8-508.

(d) An entitlement holder's property interest with respect to a particular financial asset under subsection (a) of this section may be enforced against a purchaser of the financial asset or interest therein only if:

(1) Insolvency proceedings have been initiated by or against the securities intermediary;

(2) The securities intermediary does not have sufficient interests in the financial asset to satisfy the security entitlements of all of its entitlement holders to that financial asset;

(3) The securities intermediary violated its obligations under G.S. 25-8-504 by transferring the financial asset or interest therein to the purchaser; and

(4) The purchaser is not protected under subsection (e) of this section.

The trustee or other liquidator, acting on behalf of all entitlement holders having security entitlements with respect to a particular financial asset, may recover the financial asset, or interest therein, from the purchaser. If the trustee or other liquidator elects not to pursue that right, an entitlement holder whose security entitlement remains unsatisfied has the right to recover its interest in the financial asset from the purchaser.

(e) An action based on the entitlement holder's property interest with respect to a particular financial asset under subsection (a) of this section, whether framed in conversion, replevin, constructive trust, equitable lien, or other theory, may not be asserted against any purchaser of a financial asset or interest therein who gives value, obtains control, and does not act in collusion with the securities intermediary in violating the securities intermediary's obligations under G.S. 25-8-504. (1997-181, s. 1.)

§ 25-8-504. Duty of securities intermediary to maintain financial asset.

(a) A securities intermediary shall promptly obtain and thereafter maintain a financial asset in a quantity corresponding to the aggregate of all security entitlements it has established in favor of its entitlement holders with respect to that financial asset. The securities intermediary may maintain those financial assets directly or through one or more other securities intermediaries.

(b) Except to the extent otherwise agreed by its entitlement holder, a securities intermediary may not grant any security interests in a financial asset it is obligated to maintain pursuant to subsection (a) of this section.

(c) A securities intermediary satisfies the duty in subsection (a) of this section if:

(1) The securities intermediary acts with respect to the duty as agreed upon by the entitlement holder and the securities intermediary; or

(2) In the absence of agreement, the securities intermediary exercises due care in accordance with reasonable commercial standards to obtain and maintain the financial asset.

(d) This section does not apply to a clearing corporation that is itself the obligor of an option or similar obligation to which its entitlement holders have security entitlements. (1997-181, s. 1.)

§ 25-8-505. Duty of securities intermediary with respect to payments and distributions.

(a) A securities intermediary shall take action to obtain a payment or distribution made by the issuer of a financial asset. A securities intermediary satisfies the duty if:

(1) The securities intermediary acts with respect to the duty as agreed upon by the entitlement holder and the securities intermediary; or

(2) In the absence of agreement, the securities intermediary exercises due care in accordance with reasonable commercial standards to attempt to obtain the payment or distribution.

(b) A securities intermediary is obligated to its entitlement holder for a payment or distribution made by the issuer of a financial asset if the payment or distribution is received by the securities intermediary. (1997-181, s. 1.)

§ 25-8-506. Duty of securities intermediary to exercise rights as directed by entitlement holder.

A securities intermediary shall exercise rights with respect to a financial asset if directed to do so by an entitlement holder. A securities intermediary satisfies the duty if:

(1) The securities intermediary acts with respect to the duty as agreed upon by the entitlement holder and the securities intermediary; or

(2) In the absence of agreement, the securities intermediary either places the entitlement holder in a position to exercise the rights directly or exercises due care in accordance with reasonable commercial standards to follow the direction of the entitlement holder. (1997-181, s. 1.)

§ 25-8-507. Duty of securities intermediary to comply with entitlement order.

(a) A securities intermediary shall comply with an entitlement order if the entitlement order is originated by the appropriate person, the securities intermediary has had reasonable opportunity to assure itself that the entitlement order is genuine and authorized, and the securities intermediary has had reasonable opportunity to comply with the entitlement order. A securities intermediary satisfies the duty if:

(1)   The securities intermediary acts with respect to the duty as agreed upon by the entitlement holder and the securities intermediary; or

(2)   In the absence of agreement, the securities intermediary exercises due care in accordance with reasonable commercial standards to comply with the entitlement order.

(b)   If a securities intermediary transfers a financial asset pursuant to an ineffective entitlement order, the securities intermediary shall reestablish a security entitlement in favor of the person entitled to it, and pay or credit any payments or distributions that the person did not receive as a result of the wrongful transfer. If the securities intermediary does not reestablish a security entitlement, the securities intermediary is liable to the entitlement holder for damages. (1997-181, s. 1.)

§ 25-8-508. Duty of securities intermediary to change entitlement holder's position to other form of security holding.

A securities intermediary shall act at the direction of an entitlement holder to change a security entitlement into another available form of holding for which the entitlement holder is eligible, or to cause the financial asset to be transferred to a securities account of the entitlement holder with another securities intermediary. A securities intermediary satisfies the duty if:

(1)   The securities intermediary acts as agreed upon by the entitlement holder and the securities intermediary; or

(2)   In the absence of agreement, the securities intermediary exercises due care in accordance with reasonable commercial standards to follow the direction of the entitlement holder. (1997-181, s. 1.)

§ 25-8-509. Specification of duties of securities intermediary by other statute or regulation; manner of performance of duties of securities intermediary and exercise of rights of entitlement holder.

(a) If the substance of a duty imposed upon a securities intermediary by G.S. 25-8-504 through G.S. 25-8-508 is the subject of other statute, regulation, or rule, compliance with that statute, regulation, or rule satisfies the duty.

(b) To the extent that specific standards for the performance of the duties of a securities intermediary or the exercise of the rights of an entitlement holder are not specified by other statute, regulation, or rule or by agreement between the securities intermediary and entitlement holder, the securities intermediary shall perform its duties and the entitlement holder shall exercise its rights in a commercially reasonable manner.

(c) The obligation of a securities intermediary to perform the duties imposed by G.S. 25-8-504 through G.S. 25-8-508 is subject to:

(1) Rights of the securities intermediary arising out of a security interest under a security agreement with the entitlement holder or otherwise; and

(2) Rights of the securities intermediary under other law, regulation, rule, or agreement to withhold performance of its duties as a result of unfulfilled obligations of the entitlement holder to the securities intermediary.

(d) G.S. 25-8-504 through G.S. 25-8-508 do not require a securities intermediary to take any action that is prohibited by other statute, regulation, or rule. (1997-181, s. 1.)

§ 25-8-510. Rights of purchaser of security entitlement from entitlement holder.

(a) In a case not covered by the priority rules in Article 9 of this Chapter or the rules stated in subsection (c) of this section, an action based on an adverse claim to a financial asset or security entitlement, whether framed in conversion, replevin, constructive trust, equitable lien, or other theory, may not be asserted against a person who purchases a security entitlement, or an interest therein, from an entitlement holder if the purchaser gives value, does not have notice of the adverse claim, and obtains control.

(b) If an adverse claim could not have been asserted against an entitlement holder under G.S. 25-8-502, the adverse claim cannot be asserted against a person who purchases a security entitlement, or an interest therein, from the entitlement holder.

(c) In a case not covered by the priority rules in Article 9 of this Chapter, a purchaser for value of a security entitlement, or an interest therein, who obtains control has priority over a purchaser of a security entitlement, or an interest therein, who does not obtain control. Except as otherwise provided in subsection (d) of this section, purchasers who have control rank according to priority in time of:

(1) The purchaser's becoming the person for whom the securities account, in which the security entitlement is carried, is maintained, if the purchaser obtained control under G.S. 25-8-106(d)(1);

(2) The securities intermediary's agreement to comply with the purchaser's entitlement orders with respect to security entitlements carried or to be carried in the securities account in which the security entitlement is carried, if the purchaser obtained control under G.S. 25-8-106(d)(2); or

(3) If the purchaser obtained control through another person under G.S. 25-8-106(d)(3), the time on which priority would be based under this subsection if the other person were the secured party.

(d) A securities intermediary as purchaser has priority over a conflicting purchaser who has control unless otherwise agreed by the securities intermediary. (1997-181, s. 1; 2000-169, s. 26.)

§ 25-8-511. Priority among security interests and entitlement holders.

(a) Except as otherwise provided in subsections (b) and (c) of this section, if a securities intermediary does not have sufficient interests in a particular financial asset to satisfy both its obligations to entitlement holders who have security entitlements to that financial asset and its obligation to a creditor of the securities intermediary who has a security interest in that financial asset, the claims of entitlement holders, other than the creditor, have priority over the claim of the creditor.

(b) A claim of a creditor of a securities intermediary who has a security interest in a financial asset held by a securities intermediary has priority over claims of the securities intermediary's entitlement holders who have security entitlements with respect to that financial asset if the creditor has control over the financial asset.

(c) If a clearing corporation does not have sufficient financial assets to satisfy both its obligations to entitlement holders who have security entitlements with respect to a financial asset and its obligation to a creditor of the clearing corporation who has a security interest in that financial asset, the claim of the creditor has priority over the claims of entitlement holders. (1997-181, s. 1.)

Article 9.

Secured Transactions.

Part 1.

GENERAL PROVISIONS.

SUBPART 1. Short Title, Definitions, and General Concepts.

§ 25-9-101. Short title.

This Article may be cited as Uniform Commercial Code-Secured Transactions. (1965, c. 700, s. 1; 1975, c. 862, s. 7; 2000-169, s. 1.)

§ 25-9-102. Definitions and index of definitions.

(a) Article 9 definitions. - In this Article:

(1) "Accession" means goods that are physically united with other goods in such a manner that the identity of the original goods is not lost.

(2) "Account", except as used in "account for", means a right to payment of a monetary obligation, whether or not earned by performance, (i) for property that has been or is to be sold, leased, licensed, assigned, or otherwise disposed of, (ii) for services rendered or to be rendered, (iii) for a policy of insurance issued or to be issued, (iv) for a secondary obligation incurred or to be incurred,

(v) for energy provided or to be provided, (vi) for the use or hire of a vessel under a charter or other contract, (vii) arising out of the use of a credit or charge card or information contained on or for use with the card, or (viii) as winnings in a lottery or other game of chance operated or sponsored by a state, governmental unit of a state, or person licensed or authorized to operate the game by a state or governmental unit of a state. The term includes health-care-insurance receivables. The term does not include (i) rights to payment evidenced by chattel paper or an instrument, (ii) commercial tort claims, (iii) deposit accounts, (iv) investment property, (v) letter-of-credit rights or letters of credit, or (vi) rights to payment for money or funds advanced or sold, other than rights arising out of the use of a credit or charge card or information contained on or for use with the card.

(3)   "Account debtor" means a person obligated on an account, chattel paper, or general intangible. The term does not include persons obligated to pay a negotiable instrument, even if the instrument constitutes part of chattel paper.

(4)   "Accounting", except as used in "accounting for", means a record:

a.   Authenticated by a secured party;

b.   Indicating the aggregate unpaid secured obligations as of a date not more than 35 days earlier or 35 days later than the date of the record; and

c.   Identifying the components of the obligations in reasonable detail.

(5)   "Agricultural lien" means an interest, other than a security interest, in farm products:

a.   Which secures payment or performance of an obligation for:

1.   Goods or services furnished in connection with a debtor's farming operation; or

2.   Rent on real property leased by a debtor in connection with its farming operation;

b.   Which is created by statute in favor of a person that:

1.   In the ordinary course of its business furnished goods or services to a debtor in connection with a debtor's farming operation; or

2. Leased real property to a debtor in connection with the debtor's farming operation; and

c. Whose effectiveness does not depend on the person's possession of the personal property.

(6) "As-extracted collateral" means:

a. Oil, gas, or other minerals that are subject to a security interest that:

1. Is created by a debtor having an interest in the minerals before extraction; and

2. Attaches to the minerals as extracted; or

b. Accounts arising out of the sale at the wellhead or minehead of oil, gas, or other minerals in which the debtor had an interest before extraction.

(7) "Authenticate" means:

a. To sign; or

b. With present intent to adopt or accept a record, to attach to or logically associate with the record an electronic sound, symbol, or process.

(8) "Bank" means an organization that is engaged in the business of banking. The term includes savings banks, savings and loan associations, credit unions, and trust companies.

(9) "Cash proceeds" means proceeds that are money, checks, deposit accounts, or the like.

(10) "Certificate of title" means a certificate of title with respect to which a statute provides for the security interest in question to be indicated on the certificate as a condition or result of the security interest's obtaining priority over the rights of a lien creditor with respect to the collateral. The term includes another record maintained as an alternative to a certificate of title by the governmental unit that issues certificates of title if a statute permits the security interest in question to be indicated on the record as a condition or result of the

security interest's obtaining priority over the rights of a lien creditor with respect to the collateral.

(11) "Chattel paper" means a record or records that evidence both a monetary obligation and a security interest in specific goods, a security interest in specific goods and software used in the goods, a security interest in specific goods and license of software used in the goods, a lease of specific goods, or a lease of specific goods and license of software used in the goods. In this subdivision, "monetary obligation" means a monetary obligation secured by the goods or owed under a lease of the goods and includes a monetary obligation with respect to software used in the goods. The term does not include (i) charters or other contracts involving the use or hire of a vessel or (ii) records that evidence a right to payment arising out of the use of a credit or charge card or information contained on or for use with the card. If a transaction is evidenced by records that include an instrument or series of instruments, the group of records taken together constitutes chattel paper.

(12) "Collateral" means the property subject to a security interest or agricultural lien. The term includes:

a. Proceeds to which a security interest attaches;

b. Accounts, chattel paper, payment intangibles, and promissory notes that have been sold; and

c. Goods that are the subject of a consignment.

(13) "Commercial tort claim" means a claim arising in tort with respect to which:

a. The claimant is an organization; or

b. The claimant is an individual and the claim:

1. Arose in the course of the claimant's business or profession; and

2. Does not include damages arising out of personal injury to or the death of an individual.

(14) "Commodity account" means an account maintained by a commodity intermediary in which a commodity contract is carried for a commodity customer.

(15) "Commodity contract" means a commodity futures contract, an option on a commodity futures contract, a commodity option, or another contract if the contract or option is:

a. Traded on or subject to the rules of a board of trade that has been designated as a contract market for such a contract pursuant to federal commodities laws; or

b. Traded on a foreign commodity board of trade, exchange, or market, and is carried on the books of a commodity intermediary for a commodity customer.

(16) "Commodity customer" means a person for which a commodity intermediary carries a commodity contract on its books.

(17) "Commodity intermediary" means a person that:

a. Is registered as a futures commission merchant under federal commodities law; or

b. In the ordinary course of its business provides clearance or settlement services for a board of trade that has been designated as a contract market pursuant to federal commodities law.

(18) "Communicate" means:

a. To send a written or other tangible record;

b. To transmit a record by any means agreed upon by the persons sending and receiving the record; or

c. In the case of transmission of a record to or by a filing office, to transmit a record by any means prescribed by filing-office rule.

(19) "Consignee" means a merchant to which goods are delivered in a consignment.

(20) "Consignment" means a transaction, regardless of its form, in which a person delivers goods to a merchant for the purpose of sale and:

a. The merchant:

1. Deals in goods of that kind under a name other than the name of the person making delivery;

2. Is not an auctioneer; and

3. Is not generally known by its creditors to be substantially engaged in selling the goods of others;

b. With respect to each delivery, the aggregate value of the goods is one thousand dollars ($1,000) or more at the time of delivery;

c. The goods are not consumer goods immediately before delivery; and

d. The transaction does not create a security interest that secures an obligation.

(21) "Consignor" means a person that delivers goods to a consignee in a consignment.

(22) "Consumer debtor" means a debtor in a consumer transaction.

(23) "Consumer goods" means goods that are used or bought for use primarily for personal, family, or household purposes.

(24) "Consumer-goods transaction" means a consumer transaction in which:

a. An individual incurs an obligation primarily for personal, family, or household purposes; and

b. A security interest in consumer goods secures the obligation.

(25) "Consumer obligor" means an obligor who is an individual and who incurred the obligation as part of a transaction entered into primarily for personal, family, or household purposes.

(26) "Consumer transaction" means a transaction in which (i) an individual incurs an obligation primarily for personal, family, or household purposes, (ii) a security interest secures the obligation, and (iii) the collateral is held or acquired primarily for personal, family, or household purposes. The term includes consumer-goods transactions.

(27) "Continuation statement" means an amendment of a financing statement which:

a. Identifies, by its file number, the initial financing statement to which it relates; and

b. Indicates that it is a continuation statement for, or that it is filed to continue the effectiveness of, the identified financing statement.

(28) "Debtor" means:

a. A person having an interest, other than a security interest or other lien, in the collateral, whether or not the person is an obligor;

b. A seller of accounts, chattel paper, payment intangibles, or promissory notes; or

c. A consignee.

(29) "Deposit account" means a demand, time, savings, passbook, or similar account maintained with a bank. The term does not include investment property or accounts evidenced by an instrument.

(30) "Document" means a document of title or a receipt of the type described in G.S. 25-7-201(b).

(31) "Electronic chattel paper" means chattel paper evidenced by a record or records consisting of information stored in an electronic medium.

(32) "Encumbrance" means a right, other than an ownership interest, in real property. The term includes mortgages and other liens on real property.

(33) "Equipment" means goods other than inventory, farm products, or consumer goods.

(34) "Farm products" means goods, other than standing timber, with respect to which the debtor is engaged in a farming operation and which are:

a. Crops grown, growing, or to be grown, including:

1. Crops produced on trees, vines, and bushes; and

2. Aquatic goods produced in aquacultural operations;

b. Livestock, born or unborn, including aquatic goods produced in aquacultural operations;

c. Supplies used or produced in a farming operation; or

d. Products of crops or livestock in their unmanufactured states.

(35) "Farming operation" means raising, cultivating, propagating, fattening, grazing, or any other farming, livestock, or aquacultural operation.

(36) "File number" means the number assigned to an initial financing statement pursuant to G.S. 25-9-519(a).

(37) "Filing office" means an office designated in G.S. 25-9-501 as the place to file a financing statement.

(38) "Filing-office rule" means a rule adopted pursuant to G.S. 25-9-526.

(39) "Financing statement" means a record or records composed of an initial financing statement and any filed record relating to the initial financing statement.

(40) "Fixture filing" means the filing of a financing statement covering goods that are or are to become fixtures and satisfying G.S. 25-9-502(a) and (b). The term includes the filing of a financing statement covering goods of a transmitting utility which are or are to become fixtures.

(41) "Fixtures" means goods that have become so related to particular real property that an interest in them arises under real property law.

(42) "General intangible" means any personal property, including things in action, other than accounts, chattel paper, commercial tort claims, deposit

accounts, documents, goods, instruments, investment property, letter-of-credit rights, letters of credit, money, and oil, gas, or other minerals before extraction. The term includes payment intangibles and software.

(43)　Repealed by Session Laws 2006-112, s. 21, effective October 1, 2006.

(44)　"Goods" means all things that are movable when a security interest attaches. The term includes (i) fixtures, (ii) standing timber that is to be cut and removed under a conveyance or contract for sale, (iii) the unborn young of animals, (iv) crops grown, growing, or to be grown, even if the crops are produced on trees, vines, or bushes, and (v) manufactured homes. The term also includes a computer program embedded in goods and any supporting information provided in connection with a transaction relating to the program if (i) the program is associated with the goods in such a manner that it customarily is considered part of the goods, or (ii) by becoming the owner of the goods, a person acquires a right to use the program in connection with the goods. The term does not include a computer program embedded in goods that consist solely of the medium in which the program is embedded. The term also does not include accounts, chattel paper, commercial tort claims, deposit accounts, documents, general intangibles, instruments, investment property, letter-of-credit rights, letters of credit, money, or oil, gas, or other minerals before extraction.

(45)　"Governmental unit" means a subdivision, agency, department, county, parish, municipality, or other unit of the government of the United States, a state, or a foreign country. The term includes an organization having a separate corporate existence if the organization (i) is eligible to issue debt on which interest is exempt from income taxation under the laws of the United States, or (ii) was created to facilitate the issuance of notes, bonds, other evidences of indebtedness or payment obligations for borrowed money by, or in conjunction with, installment or lease purchase financings for, this State or any county, municipality, or other agency or political subdivision thereof as evidenced by the documents creating the organization.

(46)　"Health-care-insurance receivable" means an interest in or claim under a policy of insurance which is a right to payment of a monetary obligation for health-care goods or services provided.

(47)　"Instrument" means a negotiable instrument or any other writing that evidences a right to the payment of a monetary obligation, is not itself a security agreement or lease, and is of a type that in ordinary course of business is transferred by delivery with any necessary indorsement or assignment. The term does not include (i) investment property, (ii) letters of credit, or (iii) writings that evidence a right to payment arising out of the use of a credit or charge card or information contained on or for use with the card.

(48) "Inventory" means goods, other than farm products, which:

a. Are leased by a person as lessor;

b. Are held by a person for sale or lease or to be furnished under a contract of service;

c. Are furnished by a person under a contract of service; or

d. Consist of raw materials, work in process, or materials used or consumed in a business.

(49) "Investment property" means a security, whether certificated or uncertificated, security entitlement, securities account, commodity contract, or commodity account.

(50) "Jurisdiction of organization", with respect to a registered organization, means the jurisdiction under whose law the organization is formed or organized.

(51) "Letter-of-credit right" means a right to payment or performance under a letter of credit, whether or not the beneficiary has demanded or is at the time entitled to demand payment or performance. The term does not include the right of a beneficiary to demand payment or performance under a letter of credit.

(52) "Lien creditor" means:

a. A creditor that has acquired a lien on the property involved by attachment, levy, or the like;

b. An assignee for benefit of creditors from the time of assignment;

c. A trustee in bankruptcy from the date of the filing of the petition; or

d. A receiver in equity from the time of appointment.

(53) "Manufactured home" means a structure, transportable in one or more sections, which, in the traveling mode, is eight body feet or more in width or 40 body feet or more in length, or, when erected on site, is 320 or more square feet, and which is built on a permanent chassis and designed to be used as a dwelling with or without a permanent foundation when connected to the required utilities, and includes the plumbing, heating, air-conditioning, and electrical systems contained therein. The term includes any structure that meets all of the requirements of this subdivision except the size requirements and with respect to which the manufacturer voluntarily files a certification required by the United States Secretary of Housing and Urban Development and complies with the standards established under Title 42 of the United States Code.

(54) "Manufactured-home transaction" means a secured transaction:

a. That creates a purchase-money security interest in a manufactured home, other than a manufactured home held as inventory; or

b. In which a manufactured home, other than a manufactured home held as inventory, is the primary collateral.

(55) "Mortgage" means a consensual interest in real property, including fixtures, which secures payment or performance of an obligation.

(56) "New debtor" means a person that becomes bound as debtor under G.S. 25-9-203(d) by a security agreement previously entered into by another person.

(57) "New value" means (i) money, (ii) money's worth in property, services, or new credit, or (iii) release by a transferee of an interest in property previously transferred to the transferee. The term does not include an obligation substituted for another obligation.

(58) "Noncash proceeds" means proceeds other than cash proceeds.

(59) "Obligor" means a person that, with respect to an obligation secured by a security interest in or an agricultural lien on the collateral, (i) owes payment or other performance of the obligation, (ii) has provided property other than the collateral to secure payment or other performance of the obligation, or (iii) is otherwise accountable in whole or in part for payment or other performance of the obligation. The term does not include issuers or nominated persons under a letter of credit.

(60) "Original debtor", except as used in G.S. 25-9-310(c), means a person that, as debtor, entered into a security agreement to which a new debtor has become bound under G.S. 25-9-203(d).

(61) "Payment intangible" means a general intangible under which the account debtor's principal obligation is a monetary obligation.

(62) "Person related to", with respect to an individual, means:

a. The spouse of the individual;

b. A brother, brother-in-law, sister, or sister-in-law of the individual;

c. An ancestor or lineal descendant of the individual or the individual's spouse; or

d. Any other relative, by blood or marriage, of the individual or the individual's spouse who shares the same home with the individual.

(63) "Person related to", with respect to an organization, means:

a. A person directly or indirectly controlling, controlled by, or under common control with the organization;

b. An officer or director of, or a person performing similar functions with respect to, the organization;

c. An officer or director of, or a person performing similar functions with respect to, a person described in sub-subdivision a. of this subdivision;

d. The spouse of an individual described in sub-subdivision a., b., or c. of this subdivision; or

e. An individual who is related by blood or marriage to an individual described in sub-subdivision a., b., c., or d. of this subdivision and shares the same home with the individual.

(64) "Proceeds", except as used in G.S. 25-9-609(b), means the following property:

a. Whatever is acquired upon the sale, lease, license, exchange, or other disposition of collateral;

b. Whatever is collected on, or distributed on account of, collateral;

c. Rights arising out of collateral;

d. To the extent of the value of collateral, claims arising out of the loss, nonconformity, or interference with the use of, defects or infringement of rights in, or damage to, the collateral; or

e. To the extent of the value of collateral and to the extent payable to the debtor or the secured party, insurance payable by reason of the loss or nonconformity of, defects or infringement of rights in, or damage to, the collateral.

(65) "Production-money crops" means crops that secure a production-money obligation incurred with respect to the production of those crops.

(66) "Production-money obligation" means an obligation of an obligor incurred for new value given to enable the debtor to produce crops if the value is in fact used for the production of the crops.

(67) "Production of crops" includes tilling and otherwise preparing land for growing, planting, cultivating, fertilizing, irrigating, harvesting, gathering, and curing crops, and protecting them from damage or disease.

(68) "Promissory note" means an instrument that evidences a promise to pay a monetary obligation, does not evidence an order to pay, and does not contain an acknowledgment by a bank that the bank has received for deposit a sum of money or funds.

(69) "Proposal" means a record authenticated by a secured party which includes the terms on which the secured party is willing to accept collateral in full or partial satisfaction of the obligation it secures pursuant to G.S. 25-9-620, 25-9-621, and 25-9-622.

(70) "Public-finance transaction" means a secured transaction in connection with which:

a. Debt securities are issued;

b. All or a portion of the securities issued have an initial stated maturity of at least 20 years; and

c. The debtor, obligor, secured party, account debtor or other person obligated on collateral, assignor or assignee of a secured obligation, or assignor or assignee of a security interest is a state or a governmental unit of a state.

(70a) "Public organic record" means a record that is available to the public for inspection and is:

a. A record consisting of the record initially filed with or issued by a state or the United States to form or organize an organization and any record filed with or issued by the state or the United States which amends or restates the initial record;

b. An organic record of a business trust consisting of the record initially filed with a state and any record filed with the state which amends or restates the initial record, if a statute of the state governing business trusts requires that the record be filed with the state; or

c. A record consisting of legislation enacted by the legislature of a state or the Congress of the United States which forms or organizes an organization, any record amending the legislation, and any record filed with or issued by the state or the United States which amends or restates the name of the organization.

(71) "Pursuant to commitment", with respect to an advance made or other value given by a secured party, means pursuant to the secured party's obligation, whether or not a subsequent event of default or other event not within the secured party's control has relieved or may relieve the secured party from its obligation.

(72) "Record", except as used in "for record", "of record", "record or legal title", and "record owner", means information that is inscribed on a tangible medium or that is stored in an electronic or other medium and is retrievable in perceivable form.

(73) "Registered organization" means an organization formed or organized solely under the law of a single state or the United States by the filing of a public organic record with, the issuance of a public organic record by, or the enactment

of legislation by the state or the United States. The term includes a business trust that is formed or organized under the law of a single state if a statute of the state governing business trusts requires that the business trust's organic record be filed with the state.

(74) "Secondary obligor" means an obligor to the extent that:

a. The obligor's obligation is secondary; or

b. The obligor has a right of recourse with respect to an obligation secured by collateral against the debtor, another obligor, or property of either.

(75) "Secured party" means:

a. A person in whose favor a security interest is created or provided for under a security agreement, whether or not any obligation to be secured is outstanding;

b. A person that holds an agricultural lien;

c. A consignor;

d. A person to which accounts, chattel paper, payment intangibles, or promissory notes have been sold;

e. A trustee, indenture trustee, agent, collateral agent, or other representative in whose favor a security interest or agricultural lien is created or provided for; or

f. A person that holds a security interest arising under G.S. 25-2-401, 25-2-505, 25-2-711(3), 25-2A-508(5), 25-4-208, or 25-5-118.

(76) "Security agreement" means an agreement that creates or provides for a security interest.

(77) "Send", in connection with a record or notification, means:

a. To deposit in the mail, deliver for transmission, or transmit by any other usual means of communication, with postage or cost of transmission provided for, addressed to any address reasonable under the circumstances; or

b. To cause the record or notification to be received within the time that it would have been received if properly sent under sub-subdivision a. of this subdivision.

(78) "Software" means a computer program and any supporting information provided in connection with a transaction relating to the program. The term does not include a computer program that is included in the definition of goods.

(79) "State" means a state of the United States, the District of Columbia, Puerto Rico, the United States Virgin Islands, or any territory or insular possession subject to the jurisdiction of the United States.

(80) "Supporting obligation" means a letter-of-credit right or secondary obligation that supports the payment or performance of an account, chattel paper, a document, a general intangible, an instrument, or investment property.

(81) "Tangible chattel paper" means chattel paper evidenced by a record or records consisting of information that is inscribed on a tangible medium.

(82) "Termination statement" means an amendment of a financing statement which:

a. Identifies, by its file number, the initial financing statement to which it relates; and

b. Indicates either that it is a termination statement or that the identified financing statement is no longer effective.

(83) "Transmitting utility" means a person primarily engaged in the business of:

a. Operating a railroad, subway, street railway, or trolley bus;

b. Transmitting communications electrically, electromagnetically, or by light;

c. Transmitting goods by pipeline or sewer; or

d. Transmitting or producing and transmitting electricity, steam, gas, or water.

(b) Definitions in other articles. - "Control" as provided in G.S. 25-7-106 and the following definitions in other Articles of this Chapter apply to this Article:

"Applicant"	G.S. 25-5-102.
"Beneficiary"	G.S. 25-5-102.
"Broker"	G.S. 25-8-102.
"Certificated security"	G.S. 25-8-102.
"Check"	G.S. 25-3-104.
"Clearing corporation"	G.S. 25-8-102.
"Contract for sale"	G.S. 25-2-106.
"Customer"	G.S. 25-4-104.
"Entitlement holder"	G.S. 25-8-102.
"Financial asset"	G.S. 25-8-102.
"Holder in due course"	G.S. 25-3-302.
"Issuer" (with respect to a letter of credit or letter-of-credit right)	G.S. 25-5-102.
"Issuer" (with respect to a security)	G.S. 25-8-201.
"Issuer" (with respect to documents of title)	G.S. 25-7-102.
"Lease"	G.S. 25-2A-103.
"Lease agreement"	G.S. 25-2A-103.
"Lease contract"	G.S. 25-2A-103.

"Leasehold interest"	G.S. 25-2A-103.
"Lessee"	G.S. 25-2A-103.
"Lessee in ordinary course of business"	G.S. 25-2A-103.
"Lessor"	G.S. 25-2A-103.
"Lessor's residual interest"	G.S. 25-2A-103.
"Letter of credit"	G.S. 25-5-102.
"Merchant"	G.S. 25-2-104.
"Negotiable instrument"	G.S. 25-3-104.
"Nominated person"	G.S. 25-5-102.
"Note"	G.S. 25-3-104.
"Proceeds of a letter of credit"	G.S. 25-5-114.
"Prove"	G.S. 25-3-103.
"Sale"	G.S. 25-2-106.
"Securities account"	G.S. 25-8-501.
"Securities intermediary"	G.S. 25-8-102.
"Security"	G.S. 25-8-102.
"Security certificate"	G.S. 25-8-102.
"Security entitlement"	G.S. 25-8-102.

"Uncertificated security" G.S. 25-8-102.

(c) Article 1 definitions and principles. - Article 1 of this Chapter contains general definitions and principles of construction and interpretation applicable throughout this Article. (1965, c. 700, s. 1; 1967, c. 562, s. 1; 1975, c. 862, s. 7; 1989 (Reg. Sess., 1990), c. 1024, s. 8(g); 1997-181, s. 3; 1997-456, s. 4; 1999-73, s. 6; 2000-169, s. 1; 2001-218, s. 1; 2006-112, ss. 21, 44; 2012-70, s. 1.)

§ 25-9-103. Purchase-money security interest; application of payments; burden of establishing.

(a) Definitions. - In this section:

(1) "Purchase-money collateral" means goods or software that secures a purchase-money obligation incurred with respect to that collateral; and

(2) "Purchase-money obligation" means an obligation of an obligor incurred as all or part of the price of the collateral or for value given to enable the debtor to acquire rights in or the use of the collateral if the value is in fact so used.

(b) Purchase-money security interest in goods. - A security interest in goods is a purchase-money security interest:

(1) To the extent that the goods are purchase-money collateral with respect to that security interest;

(2) If the security interest is in inventory that is or was purchase-money collateral, also to the extent that the security interest secures a purchase-money obligation incurred with respect to other inventory in which the secured party holds or held a purchase-money security interest; and

(3) Also to the extent that the security interest secures a purchase-money obligation incurred with respect to software in which the secured party holds or held a purchase-money security interest.

(c) Purchase-money security interest in software. - A security interest in software is a purchase-money security interest to the extent that the security interest also secures a purchase-money obligation incurred with respect to goods in which the secured party holds or held a purchase-money security interest if:

(1) The debtor acquired its interest in the software in an integrated transaction in which it acquired an interest in the goods; and

(2) The debtor acquired its interest in the software for the principal purpose of using the software in the goods.

(d) Consignor's inventory purchase-money security interest. - The security interest of a consignor in goods that are the subject of a consignment is a purchase-money security interest in inventory.

(e) Application of payment in non-consumer-goods transaction. - In a transaction other than a consumer-goods transaction, if the extent to which a security interest is a purchase-money security interest depends on the application of a payment to a particular obligation, the payment must be applied:

(1) In accordance with any reasonable method of application to which the parties agree;

(2) In the absence of the parties' agreement to a reasonable method, in accordance with any intention of the obligor manifested at or before the time of payment; or

(3) In the absence of an agreement to a reasonable method and a timely manifestation of the obligor's intention, in the following order:

a. To obligations that are not secured; and

b. If more than one obligation is secured, to obligations secured by purchase-money security interests in the order in which those obligations were incurred.

(f) No loss of status of purchase-money security interest in non-consumer-goods transaction. - In a transaction other than a consumer-goods transaction, a purchase-money security interest does not lose its status as such, even if:

(1) The purchase-money collateral also secures an obligation that is not a purchase-money obligation;

(2) Collateral that is not purchase-money collateral also secures the purchase-money obligation; or

(3) The purchase-money obligation has been renewed, refinanced, consolidated, or restructured.

(g) Burden of proof in non-consumer-goods transaction. - In a transaction other than a consumer-goods transaction, a secured party claiming a purchase-money security interest has the burden of establishing the extent to which the security interest is a purchase-money security interest.

(h) Non-consumer-goods transactions; no inference. - The limitation of the rules in subsections (e), (f), and (g) of this section to transactions other than consumer-goods transactions is intended to leave to the court the determination of the proper rules in consumer-goods transactions. The court may not infer from that limitation the nature of the proper rule in consumer-goods transactions and may continue to apply established approaches. (1965, c. 700, s. 1; 1975, c. 862, s. 7; 1993, c. 370, s. 1; 2000-169, s. 1.)

§ 25-9-103.1. Production-money crops; production-money obligation; production-money security interest; burden of establishing.

(a) Production-money crops. - A security interest in crops is a production-money security interest to the extent that the crops are production-money crops.

(b) Production-money obligation. - If the extent to which a security interest is a production-money security interest depends on the application of a payment to a particular obligation, the payment must be applied:

(1) In accordance with any reasonable method of application to which the parties agree;

(2) In the absence of the parties' agreement to a reasonable method, in accordance with any intention of the obligor manifested at or before the time of payment; or

(3) In the absence of an agreement to a reasonable method and a timely manifestation of the obligor's intention, in the following order:

a. To obligations that are not secured; and

b. If more than one obligation is secured, to obligations secured by production-money security interests in the order in which those obligations were incurred.

(c) Production-money security interest. - A production-money security interest does not lose its status as such, even if:

(1) The production-money crops also secure an obligation that is not a production-money obligation;

(2) Collateral that is not production-money crops also secures the production-money obligation; or

(3) The production-money obligation has been renewed, refinanced, or restructured.

(d) Burden of proof. - A secured party claiming a production-money security interest has the burden of establishing the extent to which the security interest is a production-money security interest. (1866-7, c. 1, s. 1; 1872-3, c. 133, s. 1; Code, s. 1799; 1893, c. 9; Rev., s. 2052; C.S., s. 2480; 1925, c. 302, s. 1; 1927, c. 22; 1935, c. 205; 1945, c. 196, s. 4; 1955, c. 816; 1957, c. 999; 1965, c. 700, s. 1; 1967, c. 24, s. 13; 1975, c. 862, s. 7; 1979, c. 404, s. 2; 1989 (Reg. Sess., 1990), c. 1024, s. 8(o); 1997-181, ss. 15, 16; 1997-336, s. 1; 1997-456, s. 5; 2000-169, s. 1.)

§ 25-9-104. Control of deposit account.

(a) Requirements for control. - A secured party has control of a deposit account if:

(1) The secured party is the bank with which the deposit account is maintained;

(2) The debtor, secured party, and bank have agreed in an authenticated record that the bank will comply with instructions originated by the secured party directing disposition of the funds in the deposit account without further consent by the debtor; or

(3) The secured party becomes the bank's customer with respect to the deposit account.

(b) Debtor's right to direct disposition. - A secured party that has satisfied subsection (a) of this section has control, even if the debtor retains the right to direct the disposition of funds from the deposit account. (1965, c. 700, s. 1; 1975, c. 862, s. 7; 1999-73, s. 5(a), (b); 2000-169, s. 1.)

§ 25-9-105. Control of electronic chattel paper.

(a) General Rule: Control of Electronic Chattel Paper. - A secured party has control of electronic chattel paper if a system employed for evidencing the transfer of interests in the chattel paper reliably establishes the secured party as the person to which the chattel paper was assigned.

(b) Specific Facts Giving Control. - A system satisfies subsection (a) of this section if the record or records comprising the chattel paper are created, stored, and assigned in such a manner that:

(1) A single authoritative copy of the record or records exists which is unique, identifiable, and, except as otherwise provided in subdivisions (4), (5), and (6) of this section, unalterable;

(2) The authoritative copy identifies the secured party as the assignee of the record or records;

(3) The authoritative copy is communicated to and maintained by the secured party or its designated custodian;

(4) Copies or amendments that add or change an identified assignee of the authoritative copy can be made only with the consent of the secured party;

(5) Each copy of the authoritative copy and any copy of a copy is readily identifiable as a copy that is not the authoritative copy; and

(6) Any amendment of the authoritative copy is readily identifiable as authorized or unauthorized. (1965, c. 700, s. 1; 1967, c. 562, s. 1; 1975, c. 862,

s. 7; 1989 (Reg. Sess., 1990), c. 1024, s. 8(g); 1997-181, s. 3; 1997-456, s. 4; 1999-73, s. 6; 2000-169, s. 1; 2012-70, s. 2.)

§ 25-9-106. Control of investment property.

(a) Control under G.S. 25-8-106. - A person has control of a certificated security, uncertificated security, or security entitlement as provided in G.S. 25-8-106.

(b) Control of commodity contract. - A secured party has control of a commodity contract if:

(1) The secured party is the commodity intermediary with which the commodity contract is carried; or

(2) The commodity customer, secured party, and commodity intermediary have agreed that the commodity intermediary will apply any value distributed on account of the commodity contract as directed by the secured party without further consent by the commodity customer.

(c) Effect of control of securities account or commodity account. - A secured party having control of all security entitlements or commodity contracts carried in a securities account or commodity account has control over the securities account or commodity account. (1945, c. 196, s. 1; 1957, c. 504; 1965, c. 700, s. 1; 1967, c. 562, s. 1; 1975, c. 862, s. 7; 1997-181, s. 4; 1999-73, s. 7; 2000-169, s. 1.)

§ 25-9-107. Control of letter-of-credit right.

A secured party has control of a letter-of-credit right to the extent of any right to payment or performance by the issuer or any nominated person if the issuer or nominated person has consented to an assignment of proceeds of the letter of credit under G.S. 25-5-114(c) or otherwise applicable law or practice. (1965, c. 700, s. 1; 1975, c. 862, s. 7; 1993, c. 370, s. 1; 2000-169, s. 1.)

§ 25-9-108. Sufficiency of description.

(a) Sufficiency of description. - Except as otherwise provided in subsections (c), (d), and (e) of this section, a description of personal or real property is sufficient, whether or not it is specific, if it reasonably identifies what is described.

(b) Examples of reasonable identification. - Except as otherwise provided in subsection (d) of this section, a description of collateral reasonably identifies the collateral if it identifies the collateral by:

(1) Specific listing;

(2) Category;

(3) Except as otherwise provided in subsection (e) of this section, a type of collateral defined in this Chapter;

(4) Quantity;

(5) Computational or allocational formula or procedure; or

(6) Except as otherwise provided in subsection (c) of this section, any other method, if the identity of the collateral is objectively determinable.

(c) Supergeneric description not sufficient. - A description of collateral as "all the debtor's assets" or "all the debtor's personal property" or using words of similar import does not reasonably identify the collateral.

(d) Investment property. - Except as otherwise provided in subsection (e) of this section, a description of a security entitlement, securities account, or commodity account is sufficient if it describes:

(1) The collateral by those terms or as investment property; or

(2) The underlying financial asset or commodity contract.

(e) When description by type insufficient. - A description only by type of collateral defined in this Chapter is an insufficient description of:

(1) A commercial tort claim; or

(2) In a consumer transaction, consumer goods, a security entitlement, a securities account, or a commodity account. (1965, c. 700, s. 1; 1975, c. 862, s. 7; 2000-169, s. 1.)

2. Applicability of Article.

§ 25-9-109. Scope.

(a) General scope of Article. - Except as otherwise provided in subsections (c) and (d) of this section, this Article applies to:

(1) A transaction, regardless of its form, that creates a security interest in personal property or fixtures by contract;

(2) An agricultural lien;

(3) A sale of accounts, chattel paper, payment intangibles, or promissory notes;

(4) A consignment;

(5) A security interest arising under G.S. 25-2-401, 25-2-505, 25-2-711(3), or 25-2A-508(5), as provided in G.S. 25-9-110; and

(6) A security interest arising under G.S. 25-4-208 or G.S. 25-5-118.

(b) Security interest in secured obligation. - The application of this Article to a security interest in a secured obligation is not affected by the fact that the obligation is itself secured by a transaction or interest to which this Article does not apply.

(c) Extent to which Article does not apply. - This Article does not apply to the extent that:

(1) A statute, regulation, or treaty of the United States preempts this Article;

(2) Repealed by Session Laws 2001-218, s. 2.

(3) A statute of another state, a foreign country, or a governmental unit of another state or a foreign country, other than a statute generally applicable to security interests, expressly governs creation, perfection, priority, or enforcement of a security interest created by the state, country, or governmental unit; or

(4) The rights of a transferee beneficiary or nominated person under a letter of credit are independent and superior under G.S. 25-5-114.

(d) Inapplicability of Article. - This Article does not apply to:

(1) A landlord's lien, other than an agricultural lien;

(2) A lien, other than an agricultural lien, given by statute or other rule of law for services or materials, but G.S. 25-9-333 applies with respect to priority of the lien;

(3) An assignment of a claim for wages, salary, or other compensation of an employee;

(4) A sale of accounts, chattel paper, payment intangibles, or promissory notes as part of a sale of the business out of which they arose;

(5) An assignment of accounts, chattel paper, payment intangibles, or promissory notes which is for the purpose of collection only;

(6) An assignment of a right to payment under a contract to an assignee that is also obligated to perform under the contract;

(7) An assignment of a single account, payment intangible, or promissory note to an assignee in full or partial satisfaction of a preexisting indebtedness;

(8) A transfer of an interest in or an assignment of a claim under a policy of insurance, other than an assignment by or to a health-care provider of a health-care-insurance receivable and any subsequent assignment of the right to payment, but G.S. 25-9-315 and G.S. 25-9-322 apply with respect to proceeds and priorities in proceeds;

(9) An assignment of a right represented by a judgment, other than a judgment taken on a right to payment that was collateral;

(10) A right of recoupment or setoff, but:

a. G.S. 25-9-340 applies with respect to the effectiveness of rights of recoupment or setoff against deposit accounts; and

b. G.S. 25-9-404 applies with respect to defenses or claims of an account debtor;

(11) The creation or transfer of an interest in or lien on real property, including a lease or rents thereunder, except to the extent that provision is made for:

a. Liens on real property in G.S. 25-9-203 and G.S. 25-9-308;

b. Fixtures in G.S. 25-9-334;

c. Fixture filings in G.S. 25-9-501, 25-9-502, 25-9-512, 25-9-516, and 25-9-519; and

d. Security agreements covering personal and real property in G.S. 25-9-604;

(12) An assignment of a claim arising in tort, other than a commercial tort claim, but G.S. 25-9-315 and G.S. 25-9-322 apply with respect to proceeds and priorities in proceeds;

(13) An assignment of a deposit account in a consumer transaction, but G.S. 25-9-315 and G.S. 25-9-322 apply with respect to proceeds and priorities in proceeds; or

(14) The creation, perfection, priority, or enforcement of any lien on, assignment of, pledge of, or security in, any revenues, rights, funds, or other tangible or intangible assets created, made, or granted by this State or a governmental unit in this State, including the assignment of rights as secured party in security interests granted by any party subject to the provisions of this Article to this State or a governmental unit in this State, to secure, directly or indirectly, any bond, note, other evidence of indebtedness, or other payment obligations for borrowed money issued by, or in connection with, installment or lease purchase financings by, this State or a governmental unit in this State. However, notwithstanding this subdivision, this Article does apply to the creation, perfection, priority, and enforcement of security interests created by

this State or a governmental unit in this State in equipment or fixtures. (1965, c. 700, s. 1; 1975, c. 862, s. 7; 2000-169, s. 1; 2001-218, s. 2.)

§ 25-9-110. Security interests arising under Article 2 or 2A of this Chapter.

A security interest arising under G.S. 25-2-401, 25-2-505, 25-2-711(3), or 25-2A-508(5) is subject to this Article. However, until the debtor obtains possession of the goods:

(1) The security interest is enforceable, even if G.S. 25-9-203(b)(3) has not been satisfied;

(2) Filing is not required to perfect the security interest;

(3) The rights of the secured party after default by the debtor are governed by Article 2 or 2A of this Chapter; and

(4) The security interest has priority over a conflicting security interest created by the debtor. (1965, c. 700, s. 1; 1975, c. 862, s. 7; 1993, c. 463, s. 3; 2000-169, s. 1.)

§ 25-9-111: Deleted or Recodified.

§ 25-9-112: Deleted or Recodified.

§ 25-9-113: Deleted or Recodified.

§ 25-9-114: Deleted or Recodified.

§ 25-9-115: Deleted or Recodified.

§ 25-9-116: Deleted or Recodified.

Part 2. Effectiveness of Security Agreement; Attachment of Security Interest; Rights of Parties to Security Agreement.

Subpart 1. Effectiveness and Attachment.

§ 25-9-201. General effectiveness of security agreement.

(a)   General effectiveness. - Except as otherwise provided in this Chapter, a security agreement is effective according to its terms between the parties, against purchasers of the collateral, and against creditors.

(b)   Applicable consumer laws and other law. - A transaction subject to this Article is subject to any applicable rule of law which establishes a different rule for consumers, to any other statute, rule, or regulation of this State that regulates the rates, charges, agreements, and practices for loans, credit sales, or other extensions of credit, and to any consumer-protection statute, rule, or regulation of this State, including Chapter 24 of the General Statutes, the Retail Installment Sales Act (Chapter 25A of the General Statutes), the North Carolina Consumer Finance Act (Article 15 of Chapter 53 of the General Statutes), and the Pawnbrokers and Cash Converters Modernization Act (Part 1 of Article 45 of Chapter 66 of the General Statutes).

(c)   Other applicable law controls. - In case of conflict between this Article and a rule of law, statute, or regulation described in subsection (b) of this section, the rule of law, statute, or regulation controls. Failure to comply with a statute or regulation described in subsection (b) of this section has only the effect the statute or regulation specifies.

(d)   Further deference to other applicable law. - This Article does not:

(1)   Validate any rate, charge, agreement, or practice that violates a rule of law, statute, or regulation described in subsection (b) of this section; or

(2) Extend the application of the rule of law, statute, or regulation to a transaction not otherwise subject to it. (1961, c. 574; 1965, c. 700, s. 1; 1975, c. 862, s. 7; 2000-169, s. 1; 2011-325, s. 9; 2012-46, s. 24.)

§ 25-9-202. Title to collateral immaterial.

Except as otherwise provided with respect to consignments or sales of accounts, chattel paper, payment intangibles, or promissory notes, the provisions of this Article with regard to rights and obligations apply whether title to collateral is in the secured party or the debtor. (1965, c. 700, s. 1; 1975, c. 862, s. 7; 2000-169, s. 1.)

§ 25-9-203. Attachment and enforceability of security interest; proceeds; supporting obligations; formal requisites.

(a) Attachment. - A security interest attaches to collateral when it becomes enforceable against the debtor with respect to the collateral, unless an agreement expressly postpones the time of attachment.

(b) Enforceability. - Except as otherwise provided in subsections (c) through (i) of this section, a security interest is enforceable against the debtor and third parties with respect to the collateral only if:

(1) Value has been given;

(2) The debtor has rights in the collateral or the power to transfer rights in the collateral to a secured party; and

(3) One of the following conditions is met:

a. The debtor has authenticated a security agreement that provides a description of the collateral and, if the security interest covers timber to be cut, a description of the land concerned;

b. The collateral is not a certificated security and is in the possession of the secured party under G.S. 25-9-313 pursuant to the debtor's security agreement;

c. The collateral is a certificated security in registered form and the security certificate has been delivered to the secured party under G.S. 25-8-301 pursuant to the debtor's security agreement; or

d. The collateral is deposit accounts, electronic chattel paper, investment property, letter-of-credit rights, or electronic documents, and the secured party has control under G.S. 25-7-106, 25-9-104, 25-9-105, 25-9-106, or 25-9-107 pursuant to the debtor's security agreement.

(c) Other UCC provisions. - Subsection (b) of this section is subject to G.S. 25-4-208 on the security interest of a collecting bank, G.S. 25-5-118 on the security interest of a letter-of-credit issuer or nominated person, G.S. 25-9-110 on a security interest arising under Article 2 or 2A of this Chapter, and G.S. 25-9-206 on security interests in investment property.

(d) When person becomes bound by another person's security agreement. - A person becomes bound as debtor by a security agreement entered into by another person if, by operation of law other than this Article or by contract:

(1) The security agreement becomes effective to create a security interest in the person's property; or

(2) The person becomes generally obligated for the obligations of the other person, including the obligation secured under the security agreement, and acquires or succeeds to all or substantially all of the assets of the other person.

(e) Effect of new debtor becoming bound. - If a new debtor becomes bound as debtor by a security agreement entered into by another person:

(1) The agreement satisfies subdivision (b)(3) of this section with respect to existing or after-acquired property of the new debtor to the extent the property is described in the agreement; and

(2) Another agreement is not necessary to make a security interest in the property enforceable.

(f) Proceeds and supporting obligations. - The attachment of a security interest in collateral gives the secured party the rights to proceeds provided by G.S. 25-9-315 and is also attachment of a security interest in a supporting obligation for the collateral.

(g) Lien securing right to payment. - The attachment of a security interest in a right to payment or performance secured by a security interest or other lien on personal or real property is also attachment of a security interest in the security interest, mortgage, or other lien.

(h) Security entitlement carried in securities account. - The attachment of a security interest in a securities account is also attachment of a security interest in the security entitlements carried in the securities account.

(i) Commodity contracts carried in commodity account. - The attachment of a security interest in a commodity account is also attachment of a security interest in the commodity contracts carried in the commodity account. (1997-181, s. 5; 2000-169, s. 1; 2006-112, s. 45.)

§ 25-9-204. After-acquired property; future advances.

(a) After-acquired collateral. - Except as otherwise provided in subsection (b) of this section, a security agreement may create or provide for a security interest in after-acquired collateral.

(b) When after-acquired property clause not effective. - A security interest does not attach under a term constituting an after-acquired property clause to:

(1) Consumer goods, other than an accession when given as additional security, unless the debtor acquires rights in them within 10 days after the secured party gives value; or

(2) A commercial tort claim.

(c) Future advances and other value. - A security agreement may provide that collateral secures, or that accounts, chattel paper, payment intangibles, or promissory notes are sold in connection with future advances or other value, whether or not the advances or value are given pursuant to commitment. (1866-7, c. 1, s. 1; 1872-3, c. 133, s. 1; Code, s. 1799; 1893, c. 9; Rev., s. 2052; C.S., s. 2480; 1925, c. 302, s. 1; 1927, c. 22; 1935, c. 205; 1945, c. 182, s. 2; c. 196, s. 1; 1955, c. 386, s. 1; c. 816; 1957, cc. 504, 999; 1965, c. 700, s. 1; 1967, c. 562, s. 1; 1975, c. 862, s. 7; 2000-169, s. 1.)

§ 25-9-205. Use or disposition of collateral permissible.

(a) When security interest not invalid or fraudulent. - A security interest is not invalid or fraudulent against creditors solely because:

(1) The debtor has the right or ability to:

a. Use, commingle, or dispose of all or part of the collateral, including returned or repossessed goods;

b. Collect, compromise, enforce, or otherwise deal with collateral;

c. Accept the return of collateral or make repossessions; or

d. Use, commingle, or dispose of proceeds; or

(2) The secured party fails to require the debtor to account for proceeds or replace collateral.

(b) Requirements of possession not relaxed. - This section does not relax the requirements of possession if attachment, perfection, or enforcement of a security interest depends upon possession of the collateral by the secured party. (1945, c. 196, s. 7; 1965, c. 700, s. 1; 1975, c. 862, s. 7; 2000-169, s. 1.)

§ 25-9-206. Security interest arising in purchase or delivery of financial asset.

(a) Security interest when person buys through securities intermediary. - A security interest in favor of a securities intermediary attaches to a person's security entitlement if:

(1) The person buys a financial asset through the securities intermediary in a transaction in which the person is obligated to pay the purchase price to the securities intermediary at the time of the purchase; and

(2) The securities intermediary credits the financial asset to the buyer's securities account before the buyer pays the securities intermediary.

(b) Security interest secures obligation to pay for financial asset. - The security interest described in subsection (a) of this section secures the person's obligation to pay for the financial asset.

(c) Security interest in payment against delivery transaction. - A security interest in favor of a person that delivers a certificated security or other financial asset represented by a writing attaches to the security or other financial asset if:

(1) The security or other financial asset:

a. In the ordinary course of business is transferred by delivery with any necessary indorsement or assignment; and

b. Is delivered under an agreement between persons in the business of dealing with such securities or financial assets; and

(2) The agreement calls for delivery against payment.

(d) Security interest secures obligation to pay for delivery. - The security interest described in subsection (c) of this section secures the obligation to make payment for the delivery. (1997-181, s. 6; 2000-169, s. 1.)

SUBPART 2. Rights and Duties.

§ 25-9-207. Rights and duties of secured party having possession or control of collateral.

(a) Duty of care when secured party in possession. - Except as otherwise provided in subsection (d) of this section, a secured party shall use reasonable care in the custody and preservation of collateral in the secured party's possession. In the case of chattel paper or an instrument, reasonable care includes taking necessary steps to preserve rights against prior parties unless otherwise agreed.

(b) Expenses, risks, duties, and rights when secured party in possession. - Except as otherwise provided in subsection (d) of this section, if a secured party has possession of collateral:

(1) Reasonable expenses, including the cost of insurance and payment of taxes or other charges, incurred in the custody, preservation, use, or operation of the collateral are chargeable to the debtor and are secured by the collateral;

(2) The risk of accidental loss or damage is on the debtor to the extent of a deficiency in any effective insurance coverage;

(3) The secured party shall keep the collateral identifiable, but fungible collateral may be commingled; and

(4) The secured party may use or operate the collateral:

a. For the purpose of preserving the collateral or its value;

b. As permitted by an order of a court having competent jurisdiction; or

c. Except in the case of consumer goods, in the manner and to the extent agreed by the debtor.

(c) Rights and duties when secured party in possession or control. - Except as otherwise provided in subsection (d) of this section, a secured party having possession of collateral or control of collateral under G.S. 25-7-106, 25-9-104, 25-9-105, 25-9-106, or 25-9-107:

(1) May hold as additional security any proceeds, except money or funds, received from the collateral;

(2) Shall apply money or funds received from the collateral to reduce the secured obligation, unless remitted to the debtor; and

(3) May create a security interest in the collateral.

(d) Buyer of certain rights to payment. - If the secured party is a buyer of accounts, chattel paper, payment intangibles, or promissory notes or a consignor:

(1) Subsection (a) of this section does not apply unless the secured party is entitled under an agreement:

a. To charge back uncollected collateral; or

b. Otherwise to full or limited recourse against the debtor or a secondary obligor based on the nonpayment or other default of an account debtor or other obligor on the collateral; and

(2) Subsections (b) and (c) of this section do not apply. (1965, c. 700, s. 1; 1975, c. 862, s. 7; 2000-169, s. 1; 2006-112, s. 46.)

§ 25-9-208. Additional duties of secured party having control of collateral.

(a) Applicability of section. - This section applies to cases in which there is no outstanding secured obligation and the secured party is not committed to make advances, incur obligations, or otherwise give value.

(b) Duties of secured party after receiving demand from debtor. - Within 10 days after receiving an authenticated demand by the debtor:

(1) A secured party having control of a deposit account under G.S. 25-9-104(a)(2) shall send to the bank with which the deposit account is maintained an authenticated statement that releases the bank from any further obligation to comply with instructions originated by the secured party;

(2) A secured party having control of a deposit account under G.S. 25-9-104(a)(3) shall:

a. Pay the debtor the balance on deposit in the deposit account; or

b. Transfer the balance on deposit into a deposit account in the debtor's name;

(3) A secured party, other than a buyer, having control of electronic chattel paper under G.S. 25-9-105 shall:

a. Communicate the authoritative copy of the electronic chattel paper to the debtor or its designated custodian;

b. If the debtor designates a custodian that is the designated custodian with which the authoritative copy of the electronic chattel paper is maintained for the secured party, communicate to the custodian an authenticated record releasing the designated custodian from any further obligation to comply with instructions originated by the secured party and instructing the custodian to comply with instructions originated by the debtor; and

c. Take appropriate action to enable the debtor or its designated custodian to make copies of or revisions to the authoritative copy which add or change an identified assignee of the authoritative copy without the consent of the secured party;

(4) A secured party having control of investment property under G.S. 25-8-106(d)(2) or G.S. 25-9-106(b) shall send to the securities intermediary or commodity intermediary with which the security entitlement or commodity contract is maintained an authenticated record that releases the securities intermediary or commodity intermediary from any further obligation to comply with entitlement orders or directions originated by the secured party;

(5) A secured party having control of a letter-of-credit right under G.S. 25-9-107 shall send to each person having an unfulfilled obligation to pay or deliver proceeds of the letter of credit to the secured party an authenticated release from any further obligation to pay or deliver proceeds of the letter of credit to the secured party; and

(6) A secured party having control of an electronic document shall:

a. Give control of the electronic document to the debtor or its designated custodian;

b. If the debtor designates a custodian that is the designated custodian with which the authoritative copy of the electronic document is maintained for the secured party, communicate to the custodian an authenticated record releasing the designated custodian from any further obligation to comply with instructions originated by the secured party and instructing the custodian to comply with instructions originated by the debtor; and

c. Take appropriate action to enable the debtor or its designated custodian to make copies of or revisions to the authoritative copy which add or change an identified assignee of the authoritative copy without the consent of the secured party. (2000-169, s. 1; 2006-112, s. 47.)

§ 25-9-209. Duties of secured party if account debtor has been notified of assignment.

(a)   Applicability of section. - Except as otherwise provided in subsection (c) of this section, this section applies if:

(1)   There is no outstanding secured obligation; and

(2)   The secured party is not committed to make advances, incur obligations, or otherwise give value.

(b)   Duties of secured party after receiving demand from debtor. - Within 10 days after receiving an authenticated demand by the debtor, a secured party shall send to an account debtor that has received notification of an assignment to the secured party as assignee under G.S. 25-9-406(a) an authenticated record that releases the account debtor from any further obligation to the secured party.

(c)   Inapplicability to sales. - This section does not apply to an assignment constituting the sale of an account, chattel paper, or payment intangible. (2000-169, s. 1.)

§ 25-9-210. Request for accounting; request regarding list of collateral or statement of account.

(a)   Definitions. - In this section:

(1)   "Request" means a record of a type described in subdivision (2), (3), or (4) of this subsection.

(2)   "Request for an accounting" means a record authenticated by a debtor requesting that the recipient provide an accounting of the unpaid obligations secured by collateral and reasonably identifying the transaction or relationship that is the subject of the request.

(3)   "Request regarding a list of collateral" means a record authenticated by a debtor requesting that the recipient approve or correct a list of what the debtor believes to be the collateral securing an obligation and reasonably identifying the transaction or relationship that is the subject of the request.

(4) "Request regarding a statement of account" means a record authenticated by a debtor requesting that the recipient approve or correct a statement indicating what the debtor believes to be the aggregate amount of unpaid obligations secured by collateral as of a specified date and reasonably identifying the transaction or relationship that is the subject of the request.

(b) Duty to respond to requests. - Subject to subsections (c), (d), (e), and (f) of this section, a secured party, other than a buyer of accounts, chattel paper, payment intangibles, or promissory notes or a consignor, shall comply with a request within 14 days after receipt:

(1) In the case of a request for an accounting, by authenticating and sending to the debtor an accounting; and

(2) In the case of a request regarding a list of collateral or a request regarding a statement of account, by authenticating and sending to the debtor an approval or correction.

(c) Request regarding list of collateral; statement concerning type of collateral. - A secured party that claims a security interest in all of a particular type of collateral owned by the debtor may comply with a request regarding a list of collateral by sending to the debtor an authenticated record including a statement to that effect within 14 days after receipt.

(d) Request regarding list of collateral; no interest claimed. - A person that receives a request regarding a list of collateral, claims no interest in the collateral when it receives the request, and claimed an interest in the collateral at an earlier time shall comply with the request within 14 days after receipt by sending to the debtor an authenticated record:

(1) Disclaiming any interest in the collateral; and

(2) If known to the recipient, providing the name and mailing address of any assignee of or successor to the recipient's interest in the collateral.

(e) Request for accounting or regarding statement of account; no interest in obligation claimed. - A person that receives a request for an accounting or a request regarding a statement of account, claims no interest in the obligations when it receives the request, and claimed an interest in the obligations at an earlier time shall comply with the request within 14 days after receipt by sending to the debtor an authenticated record:

(1)   Disclaiming any interest in the obligations; and

(2)   If known to the recipient, providing the name and mailing address of any assignee of or successor to the recipient's interest in the obligations.

(f)   Charges for responses. - A debtor is entitled without charge to one response to a request under this section during any six-month period. The secured party may require payment of a charge not exceeding twenty-five dollars ($25.00) for each additional response. (2000-169, s. 1.)

PART 3.

PERFECTION AND PRIORITY.

SUBPART 1. Law Governing Perfection and Priority.

§ 25-9-301.   Law governing perfection and priority of security interests.

Except as otherwise provided in G.S. 25-9-303 through G.S. 25-9-306, the following rules determine the law governing perfection, the effect of perfection or nonperfection, and the priority of a security interest in collateral:

(1)   Except as otherwise provided in this section, while a debtor is located in a jurisdiction, the local law of that jurisdiction governs perfection, the effect of perfection or nonperfection, and the priority of a security interest in collateral.

(2)   While collateral is located in a jurisdiction, the local law of that jurisdiction governs perfection, the effect of perfection or nonperfection, and the priority of a possessory security interest in that collateral.

(3)   Except as otherwise provided in paragraph (4) of this section, while tangible negotiable documents, goods, instruments, money, or tangible chattel paper is located in a jurisdiction, the local law of that jurisdiction governs:

a.   Perfection of a security interest in the goods by filing a fixture filing;

b. Perfection of a security interest in timber to be cut; and

c. The effect of perfection or nonperfection and the priority of a nonpossessory security interest in the collateral.

(4) The local law of the jurisdiction in which the wellhead or minehead is located governs perfection, the effect of perfection or nonperfection, and the priority of a security interest in as-extracted collateral. (1945, c. 196, s. 2; 1957, c. 564; 1965, c. 700, s. 1; 1967, c. 562, s. 1; 1975, c. 862, s. 7; 1989 (Reg. Sess., 1990), c. 1024, s. 8(e), (f); 1997-181, s. 2; 1999-73, s. 4(a), (b); 2000-169, s. 1; 2006-112, s. 48.)

§ 25-9-302. Law governing perfection and priority of agricultural liens.

While farm products are located in a jurisdiction, the local law of that jurisdiction governs perfection, the effect of perfection or nonperfection, and the priority of an agricultural lien on the farm products. (2000-169, s. 1.)

§ 25-9-303. Law governing perfection and priority of security interests in goods covered by a certificate of title.

(a) Applicability of section. - This section applies to goods covered by a certificate of title, even if there is no other relationship between the jurisdiction under whose certificate of title the goods are covered and the goods or the debtor.

(b) When goods covered by certificate of title. - Goods become covered by a certificate of title when a valid application for the certificate of title and the applicable fee are delivered to the appropriate authority. Goods cease to be covered by a certificate of title at the earlier of the time the certificate of title ceases to be effective under the law of the issuing jurisdiction or the time the goods become covered subsequently by a certificate of title issued by another jurisdiction.

(c) Applicable law. - The local law of the jurisdiction under whose certificate of title the goods are covered governs perfection, the effect of perfection or nonperfection, and the priority of a security interest in goods covered by a certificate of title from the time the goods become covered by the certificate of title until the goods cease to be covered by the certificate of title. (1945, c. 196, s. 2; 1957, c. 564; 1965, c. 700, s. 1; 1967, c. 562, s. 1; 1975, c. 862, s. 7; 1989 (Reg. Sess., 1990), c. 1024, s. 8(e), (f); 1997-181, s. 2; 1999-73, s. 4(a), (b); 2000-169, s. 1.)

§ 25-9-304. Law governing perfection and priority of security interests in deposit accounts.

(a) Law of bank's jurisdiction governs. - The local law of a bank's jurisdiction governs perfection, the effect of perfection or nonperfection, and the priority of a security interest in a deposit account maintained with that bank.

(b) Bank's jurisdiction. - The following rules determine a bank's jurisdiction for purposes of this Part:

(1) If an agreement between the bank and the debtor governing the deposit account expressly provides that a particular jurisdiction is the bank's jurisdiction for purposes of this Part, this Article, or this Chapter, that jurisdiction is the bank's jurisdiction.

(2) If subdivision (1) of this subsection does not apply and an agreement between the bank and its customer governing the deposit account expressly provides that the agreement is governed by the law of a particular jurisdiction, that jurisdiction is the bank's jurisdiction.

(3) If neither subdivision (1) nor subdivision (2) of this subsection applies and an agreement between the bank and its customer governing the deposit account expressly provides that the deposit account is maintained at an office in a particular jurisdiction, that jurisdiction is the bank's jurisdiction.

(4) If none of subdivisions (1), (2), and (3) of this subsection applies, the bank's jurisdiction is the jurisdiction in which the office identified in an account statement as the office serving the customer's account is located.

(5) If none of subdivisions (1), (2), (3), and (4) of this subsection applies, the bank's jurisdiction is the jurisdiction in which the chief executive office of the bank is located. (1945, c. 196, s. 2; 1957, c. 564; 1965, c. 700, s. 1; 1967, c.

562, s. 1; 1975, c. 862, s. 7; 1989 (Reg. Sess., 1990), c. 1024, s. 8(e), (f); 1997-181, s. 2; 1999-73, s. 4(a), (b); 2000-169, s. 1.)

§ 25-9-305. Law governing perfection and priority of security interests in investment property.

(a)   Governing law: general rules. - Except as otherwise provided in subsection (c) of this section, the following rules apply:

(1)   While a security certificate is located in a jurisdiction, the local law of that jurisdiction governs perfection, the effect of perfection or nonperfection, and the priority of a security interest in the certificated security represented thereby.

(2)   The local law of the issuer's jurisdiction as specified in G.S. 25-8-110(d) governs perfection, the effect of perfection or nonperfection, and the priority of a security interest in an uncertificated security.

(3)   The local law of the securities intermediary's jurisdiction as specified in G.S. 25-8-110(e) governs perfection, the effect of perfection or nonperfection, and the priority of a security interest in a security entitlement or securities account.

(4)   The local law of the commodity intermediary's jurisdiction governs perfection, the effect of perfection or nonperfection, and the priority of a security interest in a commodity contract or commodity account.

(b)   Commodity intermediary's jurisdiction. - The following rules determine a commodity intermediary's jurisdiction for purposes of this Part:

(1)   If an agreement between the commodity intermediary and commodity customer governing the commodity account expressly provides that a particular jurisdiction is the commodity intermediary's jurisdiction for purposes of this Part, this Article, or this Chapter, that jurisdiction is the commodity intermediary's jurisdiction.

(2)   If subdivision (1) of this subsection does not apply and an agreement between the commodity intermediary and commodity customer governing the commodity account expressly provides that the agreement is governed by the

law of a particular jurisdiction, that jurisdiction is the commodity intermediary's jurisdiction.

(3)   If neither subdivision (1) nor subdivision (2) of this subsection applies and an agreement between the commodity intermediary and commodity customer governing the commodity account expressly provides that the commodity account is maintained at an office in a particular jurisdiction, that jurisdiction is the commodity intermediary's jurisdiction.

(4)   If none of subdivisions (1), (2), and (3) of this subsection applies, the commodity intermediary's jurisdiction is the jurisdiction in which the office identified in an account statement as the office serving the commodity customer's account is located.

(5)   If none of subdivisions (1), (2), (3), and (4) of this subsection applies, the commodity intermediary's jurisdiction is the jurisdiction in which the chief executive office of the commodity intermediary is located.

(c)   When perfection governed by law of jurisdiction where debtor located. - The local law of the jurisdiction in which the debtor is located governs:

(1)   Perfection of a security interest in investment property by filing;

(2)   Automatic perfection of a security interest in investment property created by a broker or securities intermediary; and

(3)   Automatic perfection of a security interest in a commodity contract or commodity account created by a commodity intermediary. (1945, c. 196, s. 2; 1957, c. 564; 1965, c. 700, s. 1; 1967, c. 562, s. 1; 1975, c. 862, s. 7; 1989 (Reg. Sess., 1990), c. 1024, s. 8(e), (f); 1997-181, s. 2; 1999-73, s. 4(a), (b); 2000-169, s. 1.)

§ 25-9-306. Law governing perfection and priority of security interests in letter-of-credit rights.

(a)   Governing law: issuer's or nominated person's jurisdiction. - Subject to subsection (c) of this section, the local law of the issuer's jurisdiction or a nominated person's jurisdiction governs perfection, the effect of perfection or nonperfection, and the priority of a security interest in a letter-of-credit right if the issuer's jurisdiction or nominated person's jurisdiction is a state.

(b) Issuer's or nominated person's jurisdiction. - For purposes of this Part, an issuer's jurisdiction or nominated person's jurisdiction is the jurisdiction whose law governs the liability of the issuer or nominated person with respect to the letter-of-credit right as provided in G.S. 25-5-116.

(c) When section not applicable. - This section does not apply to a security interest that is perfected only under G.S. 25-9-308(d). (1945, c. 196, s. 2; 1957, c. 564; 1965, c. 700, s. 1; 1967, c. 562, s. 1; 1975, c. 862, s. 7; 1989 (Reg. Sess., 1990), c. 1024, s. 8(e), (f); 1997-181, s. 2; 1999-73, s. 4(a), (b); 2000-169, s. 1.)

§ 25-9-307. Location of debtor.

(a) "Place of business." - In this section, "place of business" means a place where a debtor conducts its affairs.

(b) Debtor's location: general rules. - Except as otherwise provided in this section, the following rules determine a debtor's location:

(1) A debtor who is an individual is located at the individual's principal residence.

(2) A debtor that is an organization and has only one place of business is located at its place of business.

(3) A debtor that is an organization and has more than one place of business is located at its chief executive office.

(c) Limitation of applicability of subsection (b). - Subsection (b) of this section applies only if a debtor's residence, place of business, or chief executive office, as applicable, is located in a jurisdiction whose law generally requires information concerning the existence of a nonpossessory security interest to be made generally available in a filing, recording, or registration system as a condition or result of the security interest's obtaining priority over the rights of a lien creditor with respect to the collateral. If subsection (b) of this section does not apply, the debtor is located in the District of Columbia.

(d) Continuation of location: cessation of existence, etc. - A person that ceases to exist, have a residence, or have a place of business continues to be located in the jurisdiction specified by subsections (b) and (c) of this section.

(e) Location of registered organization organized under state law. - A registered organization that is organized under the law of a state is located in that state.

(f) Location of registered organization organized under federal law; bank branches and agencies. - Except as otherwise provided in subsection (i) of this section, a registered organization that is organized under the law of the United States and a branch or agency of a bank that is not organized under the law of the United States or a state are located:

(1) In the state that the law of the United States designates, if the law designates a state of location;

(2) In the state that the registered organization, branch, or agency designates, if the law of the United States authorizes the registered organization, branch, or agency to designate its state of location, including by designating its main office, home office, or other comparable office; or

(3) In the District of Columbia, if neither subdivision (1) nor subdivision (2) of this subsection applies.

(g) Continuation of location: change in status of registered organization. - A registered organization continues to be located in the jurisdiction specified by subsection (e) or (f) of this section notwithstanding:

(1) The suspension, revocation, forfeiture, or lapse of the registered organization's status as such in its jurisdiction of organization; or

(2) The dissolution, winding up, or cancellation of the existence of the registered organization.

(h) Location of United States. - The United States is located in the District of Columbia.

(i) Location of foreign bank branch or agency if licensed in only one state. - A branch or agency of a bank that is not organized under the law of the United States or a state is located in the state in which the branch or agency is licensed, if all branches and agencies of the bank are licensed in only one state.

(j) Location of foreign air carrier. - A foreign air carrier under the Federal Aviation Act of 1958, as amended, is located at the designated office of the agent upon which service of process may be made on behalf of the carrier.

(k) Section applies only to this Part. - This section applies only for purposes of this Part. (2000-169, s. 1; 2012-70, s. 3.)

SUBPART 2. Perfection.

§ 25-9-308. When security interest or agricultural lien is perfected; continuity of perfection.

(a) Perfection of security interest. - Except as otherwise provided in this section and G.S. 25-9-309, a security interest is perfected if it has attached and all of the applicable requirements for perfection in G.S. 25-9-310 through G.S. 25-9-316 have been satisfied. A security interest is perfected when it attaches if the applicable requirements are satisfied before the security interest attaches.

(b) Perfection of agricultural lien. - An agricultural lien is perfected if it has become effective and all of the applicable requirements for perfection in G.S. 25-9-310 have been satisfied. An agricultural lien is perfected when it becomes effective if the applicable requirements are satisfied before the agricultural lien becomes effective.

(c) Continuous perfection; perfection by different methods. - A security interest or agricultural lien is perfected continuously if it is originally perfected by one method under this Article and is later perfected by another method under this Article, without an intermediate period when it was unperfected.

(d) Supporting obligation. - Perfection of a security interest in collateral also perfects a security interest in a supporting obligation for the collateral.

(e) Lien securing right to payment. - Perfection of a security interest in a right to payment or performance also perfects a security interest in a security interest, mortgage, or other lien on personal or real property securing the right.

(f) Security entitlement carried in securities account. - Perfection of a security interest in a securities account also perfects a security interest in the security entitlements carried in the securities account.

(g) Commodity contract carried in commodity account. - Perfection of a security interest in a commodity account also perfects a security interest in the commodity contracts carried in the commodity account. (1997-181, s. 5; 2000-169, s. 1.)

§ 25-9-309. Security interest perfected upon attachment.

The following security interests are perfected when they attach:

(1) A purchase-money security interest in consumer goods, except as otherwise provided in G.S. 25-9-311(b) with respect to consumer goods that are subject to a statute or treaty described in G.S. 25-9-311(a);

(2) An assignment of accounts or payment intangibles which does not by itself or in conjunction with other assignments to the same assignee transfer a significant part of the assignor's outstanding accounts or payment intangibles;

(3) A sale of a payment intangible;

(4) A sale of a promissory note;

(5) A security interest created by the assignment of a health-care-insurance receivable to the provider of the health-care goods or services;

(6) A security interest arising under G.S. 25-2-401, 25-2-505, 25-2-711(3), or 25-2A-508(5), until the debtor obtains possession of the collateral;

(7) A security interest of a collecting bank arising under G.S. 25-4-208;

(8) A security interest of an issuer or nominated person arising under G.S. 25-5-118;

(9) A security interest arising in the delivery of a financial asset under G.S. 25-9-206(c);

(10) A security interest in investment property created by a broker or securities intermediary;

(11) A security interest in a commodity contract or a commodity account created by a commodity intermediary;

(12) An assignment for the benefit of all creditors of the transferor and subsequent transfers by the assignee thereunder; and

(13) A security interest created by an assignment of a beneficial interest in a decedent's estate. (1997-181, s. 5; 2000-169, s. 1.)

§ 25-9-310. When filing required to perfect security interest or agricultural lien; security interests and agricultural liens to which filing provisions do not apply.

(a) General rule: perfection by filing. - Except as otherwise provided in subsection (b) of this section and G.S. 25-9-312(b), a financing statement must be filed to perfect all security interests and agricultural liens.

(b) Exceptions: filing not necessary. - The filing of a financing statement is not necessary to perfect a security interest:

(1) That is perfected under G.S. 25-9-308(d), (e), (f), or (g);

(2) That is perfected under G.S. 25-9-309 when it attaches;

(3) In property subject to a statute, regulation, or treaty described in G.S. 25-9-311(a);

(4) In goods in possession of a bailee which is perfected under G.S. 25-9-312(d)(1) or (2);

(5) In certificated securities, documents, goods, or instruments which is perfected without filing, control, or possession under G.S. 25-9-312(e), (f), or (g);

(6) In collateral in the secured party's possession under G.S. 25-9-313;

(7) In a certificated security which is perfected by delivery of the security certificate to the secured party under G.S. 25-9-313;

(8) In deposit accounts, electronic chattel paper, electronic documents, investment property, or letter-of-credit rights which is perfected by control under G.S. 25-9-314;

(9) In proceeds which is perfected under G.S. 25-9-315; or

(10) That is perfected under G.S. 25-9-316.

(c) Assignment of perfected security interest. - If a secured party assigns a perfected security interest or agricultural lien, a filing under this Article is not required to continue the perfected status of the security interest against creditors of and transferees from the original debtor. (1866-7, s. 1; 1872-3, c. 133, s. 1; Code, s. 1799; 1893, c. 9; Rev., s. 2052; C.S., s. 2480; 1925, c. 302, s. 1; 1927, c. 22; 1935, c. 205; 1945, c. 182, s. 3; c. 196, s. 2; 1955, c. 816; 1957, cc. 564, 999; 1961, c. 574; 1965, c. 700, s. 1; 1967, c. 562, s. 1; 1975, c. 862, s. 7; 1977, c. 103; 1989 (Reg. Sess., 1990), c. 1024, s. 8(i); 1997-181, s. 92000-169, s. 1; 2001-218, s. 3; 2001-487, s. 57; 2006-112, s. 49.)

§ 25-9-311. Perfection of security interests in property subject to certain statutes, regulations, and treaties.

(a) Security interest subject to other law. - Except as otherwise provided in subsection (d) of this section, the filing of a financing statement is not necessary or effective to perfect a security interest in property subject to:

(1) A statute, regulation, or treaty of the United States whose requirements for a security interest's obtaining priority over the rights of a lien creditor with respect to the property preempt G.S. 25-9-310(a);

(2) A statute of this State covering automobiles or other goods that provides for a security interest to be indicated on a certificate of title as a condition to or result of perfection of the security interest, including G.S. 20-58 and G.S. 75A-41; or

(3) A statute of another jurisdiction which provides for a security interest to be indicated on a certificate of title as a condition or result of the security interest's obtaining priority over the rights of a lien creditor with respect to the property.

(b) Compliance with other law. - Compliance with the requirements of a statute, regulation, or treaty described in subsection (a) of this section for obtaining priority over the rights of a lien creditor is equivalent to the filing of a financing statement under this Article. Except as otherwise provided in subsection (d) of this section and G.S. 25-9-313 and G.S. 25-9-316(d) and (e) for goods covered by a certificate of title, a security interest in property subject to a statute, regulation, or treaty described in subsection (a) of this section may be perfected only by compliance with those requirements, and a security interest so perfected remains perfected notwithstanding a change in the use or transfer of possession of the collateral.

(c) Duration and renewal of perfection. - Except as otherwise provided in subsection (d) of this section and G.S. 25-9-316(d) and (e), duration and renewal of perfection of a security interest perfected by compliance with the requirements prescribed by a statute, regulation, or treaty described in subsection (a) of this section are governed by the statute, regulation, or treaty. In other respects, the security interest is subject to this Article.

(d) Inapplicability to certain inventory. - During any period in which collateral subject to a statute specified in subdivision (a)(2) of this section is inventory held for sale or lease by a person or leased by that person as lessor and that person is in the business of selling goods of that kind, this section does not apply to a security interest in that collateral created by that person. (1866-7, s. 1; 1872-3, c. 133, s. 1; Code, s. 1799; 1893, c. 9; Rev., s. 2052; C.S., s. 2480; 1925, c. 302, s. 1; 1927, c. 22; 1935, c. 205; 1945, c. 182, s. 3; c. 196, s. 2; 1955, c. 816; 1957, cc. 564, 999; 1961, c. 574; 1965, c. 700, s. 1; 1967, c. 562, s. 1; 1975, c. 862, s. 7; 1977, c. 103; 1989 (Reg. Sess., 1990), c. 1024, s. 8(i); 1997-181, s. 9; 2000-169, s. 1; 2012-70, s. 4.)

§ 25-9-312. Perfection of security interests in chattel paper, deposit accounts, documents, goods covered by documents, instruments, investment property, letter-of-credit rights, and money; perfection by permissive filing; temporary perfection without filing or transfer of possession.

(a) Perfection by filing permitted. - A security interest in chattel paper, negotiable documents, instruments, or investment property may be perfected by filing.

(b) Control or possession of certain collateral. - Except as otherwise provided in G.S. 25-9-315(c) and (d) for proceeds:

(1) A security interest in a deposit account may be perfected only by control under G.S. 25-9-314;

(2) And except as otherwise provided in G.S. 25-9-308(d), a security interest in a letter-of-credit right may be perfected only by control under G.S. 25-9-314; and

(3) A security interest in money may be perfected only by the secured party's taking possession under G.S. 25-9-313.

(c) Goods covered by negotiable document. - While goods are in the possession of a bailee that has issued a negotiable document covering the goods:

(1) A security interest in the goods may be perfected by perfecting a security interest in the document; and

(2) A security interest perfected in the document has priority over any security interest that becomes perfected in the goods by another method during that time.

(d) Goods covered by nonnegotiable document. - While goods are in the possession of a bailee that has issued a nonnegotiable document covering the goods, a security interest in the goods may be perfected by:

(1) Issuance of a document in the name of the secured party;

(2) The bailee's receipt of notification of the secured party's interest; or

(3) Filing as to the goods.

(e) Temporary perfection: new value. - A security interest in certificated securities, negotiable documents, or instruments is perfected without filing or the taking of possession or control for a period of 20 days from the time it attaches to the extent that it arises for new value given under an authenticated security agreement.

(f)　Temporary perfection: goods or documents made available to debtor. - A perfected security interest in a negotiable document or goods in possession of a bailee, other than one that has issued a negotiable document for the goods, remains perfected for 20 days without filing if the secured party makes available to the debtor the goods or documents representing the goods for the purpose of:

(1)　Ultimate sale or exchange; or

(2)　Loading, unloading, storing, shipping, transshipping, manufacturing, processing, or otherwise dealing with them in a manner preliminary to their sale or exchange.

(g)　Temporary perfection: delivery of security certificate or instrument to debtor. - A perfected security interest in a certificated security or instrument remains perfected for 20 days without filing if the secured party delivers the security certificate or instrument to the debtor for the purpose of:

(1)　Ultimate sale or exchange; or

(2)　Presentation, collection, enforcement, renewal, or registration of transfer.

(h)　Expiration of temporary perfection. - After the 20-day period specified in subsection (e), (f), or (g) of this section expires, perfection depends upon compliance with this Article. (1997-181, s. 5; 2000-169, s. 1; 2006-112, s. 50.)

§ 25-9-313. When possession by or delivery to secured party perfects security interest without filing.

(a)　Perfection by possession or delivery. - Except as otherwise provided in subsection (b) of this section, a secured party may perfect a security interest in tangible negotiable documents, goods, instruments, money, or tangible chattel paper by taking possession of the collateral. A secured party may perfect a security interest in certificated securities by taking delivery of the certificated securities under G.S. 25-8-301.

(b) Goods covered by certificate of title. - With respect to goods covered by a certificate of title issued by this State, a secured party may perfect a security interest in the goods by taking possession of the goods only in the circumstances described in G.S. 25-9-316(d).

(c) Collateral in possession of person other than debtor. - With respect to collateral other than certificated securities and goods covered by a document, a secured party takes possession of collateral in the possession of a person other than the debtor, the secured party, or a lessee of the collateral from the debtor in the ordinary course of the debtor's business, when:

(1) The person in possession authenticates a record acknowledging that it holds possession of the collateral for the secured party's benefit; or

(2) The person takes possession of the collateral after having authenticated a record acknowledging that it will hold possession of collateral for the secured party's benefit.

(d) Time of perfection by possession; continuation of perfection. - If perfection of a security interest depends upon possession of the collateral by a secured party, perfection occurs no earlier than the time the secured party takes possession and continues only while the secured party retains possession.

(e) Time of perfection by delivery; continuation of perfection. - A security interest in a certificated security in registered form is perfected by delivery when delivery of the certificated security occurs under G.S. 25-8-301 and remains perfected by delivery until the debtor obtains possession of the security certificate.

(f) Acknowledgment not required. - A person in possession of collateral is not required to acknowledge that it holds possession for a secured party's benefit.

(g) Effectiveness of acknowledgment; no duties or confirmation. - If a person acknowledges that it holds possession for the secured party's benefit:

(1) The acknowledgment is effective under subsection (c) of this section or G.S. 25-8-301(a), even if the acknowledgment violates the rights of a debtor; and

(2) Unless the person otherwise agrees or law other than this Article otherwise provides, the person does not owe any duty to the secured party and is not required to confirm the acknowledgment to another person.

(h) Secured party's delivery to person other than debtor. - A secured party having possession of collateral does not relinquish possession by delivering the collateral to a person other than the debtor or a lessee of the collateral from the debtor in the ordinary course of the debtor's business if the person was instructed before the delivery or is instructed contemporaneously with the delivery:

(1) To hold possession of the collateral for the secured party's benefit; or

(2) To redeliver the collateral to the secured party.

(i) Effect of delivery under subsection (h); no duties or confirmation. - A secured party does not relinquish possession, even if a delivery under subsection (h) of this section violates the rights of a debtor. A person to which collateral is delivered under subsection (h) of this section does not owe any duty to the secured party and is not required to confirm the delivery to another person unless the person otherwise agrees or law other than this Article otherwise provides. (1997-181, s. 5; 2000-169, s. 1; 2006-112, s. 51.)

§ 25-9-314. Perfection by control.

(a) Perfection by control. - A security interest in investment property, deposit accounts, letter-of-credit rights, electronic chattel paper, or electronic documents may be perfected by control of the collateral under G.S. 25-7-106, 25-9-104, 25-9-105, 25-9-106, or 25-9-107.

(b) Specified collateral: time of perfection by control; continuation of perfection. - A security interest in deposit accounts, electronic chattel paper, letter-of-credit rights, or electronic documents is perfected by control under G.S. 25-7-106, 25-9-104, 25-9-105, or 25-9-107 when the secured party obtains control and remains perfected by control only while the secured party retains control.

(c) Investment property: time of perfection by control; continuation of perfection. - A security interest in investment property is perfected by control under G.S. 25-9-106 from the time the secured party obtains control and remains perfected by control until:

(1)   The secured party does not have control; and

(2)   One of the following occurs:

a.   If the collateral is a certificated security, the debtor has or acquires possession of the security certificate;

b.   If the collateral is an uncertificated security, the issuer has registered or registers the debtor as the registered owner; or

c.   If the collateral is a security entitlement, the debtor is or becomes the entitlement holder. (1997-181, s. 5; 2000-169, s. 1; 2006-112, s. 52.)

§ 25-9-315. Secured party's rights on disposition of collateral and in proceeds.

(a)   Disposition of collateral: continuation of security interest or agricultural lien; proceeds. - Except as otherwise provided in this Article and in G.S. 25-2-403(2):

(1)   A security interest or agricultural lien continues in collateral notwithstanding sale, lease, license, exchange, or other disposition thereof unless the secured party authorized the disposition free of the security interest or agricultural lien; and

(2)   A security interest attaches to any identifiable proceeds of collateral.

(b)   When commingled proceeds identifiable. - Proceeds that are commingled with other property are identifiable proceeds:

(1)   If the proceeds are goods, to the extent provided by G.S. 25-9-336; and

(2)   If the proceeds are not goods, to the extent that the secured party identifies the proceeds by a method of tracing, including application of equitable principles, that is permitted under law other than this Article with respect to commingled property of the type involved.

(c) Perfection of security interest in proceeds. - A security interest in proceeds is a perfected security interest if the security interest in the original collateral was perfected.

(d) Continuation of perfection. - A perfected security interest in proceeds becomes unperfected on the twenty-first day after the security interest attaches to the proceeds unless:

(1) The following conditions are satisfied:

a. A filed financing statement covers the original collateral;

b. The proceeds are collateral in which a security interest may be perfected by filing in the office in which the financing statement has been filed; and

c. The proceeds are not acquired with cash proceeds;

(2) The proceeds are identifiable cash proceeds; or

(3) The security interest in the proceeds is perfected other than under subsection (c) of this section when the security interest attaches to the proceeds or within 20 days thereafter.

(e) When perfected security interest in proceeds becomes unperfected. - If a filed financing statement covers the original collateral, a security interest in proceeds which remains perfected under subdivision (d)(1) of this section becomes unperfected at the later of:

(1) When the effectiveness of the filed financing statement lapses under G.S. 25-9-515 or is terminated under G.S. 25-9-513; or

(2) The twenty-first day after the security interest attaches to the proceeds. (1945, c. 196, s. 8; 1961, c. 574; 1965, c. 700, s. 1; 1967, c. 562, s. 1; 1975, c. 862, s. 7; 1997-181, ss. 12, 13; 2000-169, s. 1.)

§ 25-9-316. Effect of change in governing law.

(a) General rule: effect on perfection of change in governing law. - A security interest perfected pursuant to the law of the jurisdiction designated in G.S. 25-9-301(1) or G.S. 25-9-305(c) remains perfected until the earliest of:

(1) The time perfection would have ceased under the law of that jurisdiction;

(2) The expiration of four months after a change of the debtor's location to another jurisdiction; or

(3) The expiration of one year after a transfer of collateral to a person that thereby becomes a debtor and is located in another jurisdiction.

(b) Security interest perfected or unperfected under law of new jurisdiction. - If a security interest described in subsection (a) of this section becomes perfected under the law of the other jurisdiction before the earliest time or event described in that subsection, it remains perfected thereafter. If the security interest does not become perfected under the law of the other jurisdiction before the earliest time or event, it becomes unperfected and is deemed never to have been perfected as against a purchaser of the collateral for value.

(c) Possessory security interest in collateral moved to new jurisdiction. - A possessory security interest in collateral, other than goods covered by a certificate of title and as-extracted collateral consisting of goods, remains continuously perfected if:

(1) The collateral is located in one jurisdiction and subject to a security interest perfected under the law of that jurisdiction;

(2) Thereafter the collateral is brought into another jurisdiction; and

(3) Upon entry into the other jurisdiction, the security interest is perfected under the law of the other jurisdiction.

(d) Goods covered by certificate of title from this State. - Except as otherwise provided in subsection (e) of this section, a security interest in goods covered by a certificate of title which is perfected by any method under the law of another jurisdiction when the goods become covered by a certificate of title from this State remains perfected until the security interest would have become unperfected under the law of the other jurisdiction had the goods not become so covered.

(e) When subsection (d) security interest becomes unperfected against purchasers. - A security interest described in subsection (d) of this section becomes unperfected as against a purchaser of the goods for value and is deemed never to have been perfected as against a purchaser of the goods for value if the applicable requirements for perfection under G.S. 25-9-311(b) or G.S. 25-9-313 are not satisfied before the earlier of:

(1) The time the security interest would have become unperfected under the law of the other jurisdiction had the goods not become covered by a certificate of title from this State; or

(2) The expiration of four months after the goods had become so covered.

(f) Change in jurisdiction of bank, issuer, nominated person, securities intermediary, or commodity intermediary. - A security interest in deposit accounts, letter-of-credit rights, or investment property which is perfected under the law of the bank's jurisdiction, the issuer's jurisdiction, a nominated person's jurisdiction, the securities intermediary's jurisdiction, or the commodity intermediary's jurisdiction, as applicable, remains perfected until the earlier of:

(1) The time the security interest would have become unperfected under the law of that jurisdiction; or

(2) The expiration of four months after a change of the applicable jurisdiction to another jurisdiction.

(g) Subsection (f) security interest perfected or unperfected under law of new jurisdiction. - If a security interest described in subsection (f) of this section becomes perfected under the law of the other jurisdiction before the earlier of the time or the end of the period described in that subsection, it remains perfected thereafter. If the security interest does not become perfected under the law of the other jurisdiction before the earlier of that time or the end of that period, it becomes unperfected and is deemed never to have been perfected as against a purchaser of the collateral for value.

(h) Effect on Filed Financing Statement of Change in Governing Law. - The following rules apply to collateral to which a security interest attaches within four months after the debtor changes its location to another jurisdiction:

(1) A financing statement filed before the change pursuant to the law of the jurisdiction designated in G.S. 25-9-301(1) or G.S. 25-9-305(c) is effective to

perfect a security interest in the collateral if the financing statement would have been effective to perfect a security interest in the collateral had the debtor not changed its location.

(2)   If a security interest perfected by a financing statement that is effective under subdivision (1) of this subsection becomes perfected under the law of the other jurisdiction before the earlier of the time the financing statement would have become ineffective under the law of the jurisdiction designated in G.S. 25-9-301(1) or G.S. 25-9-305(c) or the expiration of the four-month period, it remains perfected thereafter. If the security interest does not become perfected under the law of the other jurisdiction before the earlier time or event, it becomes unperfected and is deemed never to have been perfected as against a purchaser of the collateral for value.

(i)   Effect of Change in Governing Law on Financing Statement Filed Against Original Debtor. - If a financing statement naming an original debtor is filed pursuant to the law of the jurisdiction designated in G.S. 25-9-301(1) or G.S. 25-9-305(c) and the new debtor is located in another jurisdiction, the following rules apply:

(1)   The financing statement is effective to perfect a security interest in collateral acquired by the new debtor before, and within four months after, the new debtor becomes bound under G.S. 25-9-203(d), if the financing statement would have been effective to perfect a security interest in the collateral had the collateral been acquired by the original debtor.

(2)   A security interest perfected by the financing statement and which becomes perfected under the law of the other jurisdiction before the earlier of the time the financing statement would have become ineffective under the law of the jurisdiction designated in G.S. 25-9-301(1) or G.S. 25-9-305(c) or the expiration of the four-month period remains perfected thereafter. A security interest that is perfected by the financing statement but which does not become perfected under the law of the other jurisdiction before the earlier time or event becomes unperfected and is deemed never to have been perfected as against a purchaser of the collateral for value. (1945, c. 196, s. 2; 1957, c. 564; 1965, c. 700, s. 1; 1967, c. 562, s. 1; 1975, c. 862, s. 7; 1989 (Reg. Sess., 1990), c. 1024, s. 8(e), (f); 1997-181, s. 2; 1999-73, s. 4(a), (b); 2000-169, s. 1; 2012-70, s. 5(a), (b).)

Subpart 3. Priority.

§ 25-9-317. Interests that take priority over or take free of security interest or agricultural lien.

(a) Conflicting security interests and rights of lien creditors. - A security interest or agricultural lien is subordinate to the rights of:

(1) A person entitled to priority under G.S. 25-9-322; and

(2) Except as otherwise provided in subsection (e) of this section, a person that becomes a lien creditor before the earlier of the time:

a. The security interest or agricultural lien is perfected; or

b. One of the conditions specified in G.S. 25-9-203(b)(3) is met and a financing statement covering the collateral is filed.

(b) Buyers that receive delivery. - Except as otherwise provided in subsection (e) of this section, a buyer, other than a secured party, of tangible chattel paper, tangible documents, goods, instruments, or a certificated security takes free of a security interest or agricultural lien if the buyer gives value and receives delivery of the collateral without knowledge of the security interest or agricultural lien and before it is perfected.

(c) Lessees that receive delivery. - Except as otherwise provided in subsection (e) of this section, a lessee of goods takes free of a security interest or agricultural lien if the lessee gives value and receives delivery of the collateral without knowledge of the security interest or agricultural lien and before it is perfected.

(d) Licensees and buyers of certain collateral. - A licensee of a general intangible or a buyer, other than a secured party, of collateral other than tangible chattel paper, tangible documents, goods, instruments, or a certificated security takes free of a security interest if the licensee or buyer gives value without knowledge of the security interest and before it is perfected.

(e) Purchase-money security interest. - Except as otherwise provided in G.S. 25-9-320 and G.S. 25-9-321, if a person files a financing statement with respect to a purchase-money security interest before or within 20 days after the debtor receives delivery of the collateral, the security interest takes priority over the rights of a buyer, lessee, or lien creditor which arise between the time the security interest attaches and the time of filing. (1945, c. 182, s. 4; c. 196, s. 4; 1955, c. 386, s. 2; 1961, c. 574; 1965, c. 700, s. 1; 1975, c. 862, s. 7; 1979, c. 404, s. 1; 1997-181, s. 8; 2000-169, s. 1; 2006-112, s. 53; 2012-70, s. 6.)

§ 25-9-318. No interest retained in right to payment that is sold; rights and title of seller of account or chattel paper with respect to creditors and purchasers.

(a)   Seller retains no interest. - A debtor that has sold an account, chattel paper, payment intangible, or promissory note does not retain a legal or equitable interest in the collateral sold.

(b)   Deemed rights of debtor if buyer's security interest unperfected. - For purposes of determining the rights of creditors of, and purchasers for value of an account or chattel paper from, a debtor that has sold an account or chattel paper, while the buyer's security interest is unperfected, the debtor is deemed to have rights and title to the account or chattel paper identical to those the debtor sold. (2000-169, s. 1.)

§ 25-9-319. Rights and title of consignee with respect to creditors and purchasers.

(a)   Consignee has consignor's rights. - Except as otherwise provided in subsection (b) of this section, for purposes of determining the rights of creditors of, and purchasers for value of goods from, a consignee, while the goods are in the possession of the consignee, the consignee is deemed to have rights and title to the goods identical to those the consignor had or had power to transfer.

(b)   Applicability of other law. - For purposes of determining the rights of a creditor of a consignee, law other than this Article determines the rights and title of a consignee while goods are in the consignee's possession if, under this Part, a perfected security interest held by the consignor would have priority over the rights of the creditor. (2000-169, s. 1.)

§ 25-9-320. Buyer of goods.

(a) Buyer in ordinary course of business. - Except as otherwise provided in subsection (e) of this section, a buyer in ordinary course of business, other than a person buying farm products from a person engaged in farming operations, takes free of a security interest created by the buyer's seller, even if the security interest is perfected and the buyer knows of its existence.

(b) Buyer of consumer goods. - Except as otherwise provided in subsection (e) of this section, a buyer of goods from a person who used or bought the goods for use primarily for personal, family, or household purposes takes free of a security interest, even if perfected, if the buyer buys:

(1) Without knowledge of the security interest;

(2) For value;

(3) Primarily for the buyer's personal, family, or household purposes; and

(4) Before the filing of a financing statement covering the goods.

(c) Effectiveness of filing for subsection (b). - To the extent that it affects the priority of a security interest over a buyer of goods under subsection (b) of this section, the period of effectiveness of a filing made in the jurisdiction in which the seller is located is governed by G.S. 25-9-316(a) and (b).

(d) Buyer in ordinary course of business at wellhead or minehead. - A buyer in ordinary course of business buying oil, gas, or other minerals at the wellhead or minehead or after extraction takes free of an interest arising out of an encumbrance.

(e) Possessory security interest not affected. - Subsections (a) and (b) of this section do not affect a security interest in goods in the possession of the secured party under G.S. 25-9-313. (1945, c. 182, s. 4; 1955, c. 386, s. 2; 1961, c. 574; 1965, c. 700, s. 1; 1975, c. 862, s. 7.; 2000-169, s. 1.)

§ 25-9-321. Licensee of general intangible and lessee of goods in ordinary course of business.

(a) "Licensee in ordinary course of business". - In this section, "licensee in ordinary course of business" means a person that becomes a licensee of a general intangible in good faith, without knowledge that the license violates the rights of another person in the general intangible, and in the ordinary course from a person in the business of licensing general intangibles of that kind. A person becomes a licensee in the ordinary course if the license to the person comports with the usual or customary practices in the kind of business in which the licensor is engaged or with the licensor's own usual or customary practices.

(b) Rights of licensee in ordinary course of business. - A licensee in ordinary course of business takes its rights under a nonexclusive license free of a security interest in the general intangible created by the licensor, even if the security interest is perfected and the licensee knows of its existence.

(c) Rights of lessee in ordinary course of business. - A lessee in ordinary course of business takes its leasehold interest free of a security interest in the goods created by the lessor, even if the security interest is perfected and the lessee knows of its existence. (1993, c. 463, s. 1; 2000-169, s. 1.)

§ 25-9-322. Priorities among conflicting security interests in and agricultural liens on same collateral.

(a) General priority rules. - Except as otherwise provided in this section, priority among conflicting security interests and agricultural liens in the same collateral is determined according to the following rules:

(1) Conflicting perfected security interests and agricultural liens rank according to priority in time of filing or perfection. Priority dates from the earlier of the time a filing covering the collateral is first made or the security interest or agricultural lien is first perfected, if there is no period thereafter when there is neither filing nor perfection.

(2) A perfected security interest or agricultural lien has priority over a conflicting unperfected security interest or agricultural lien.

(3) The first security interest or agricultural lien to attach or become effective has priority if conflicting security interests and agricultural liens are unperfected.

(b) Time of perfection: proceeds and supporting obligations. - For the purposes of subdivision (a)(1) of this section:

(1) The time of filing or perfection as to a security interest in collateral is also the time of filing or perfection as to a security interest in proceeds; and

(2) The time of filing or perfection as to a security interest in collateral supported by a supporting obligation is also the time of filing or perfection as to a security interest in the supporting obligation.

(c) Special priority rules: proceeds and supporting obligations. - Except as otherwise provided in subsection (f) of this section, a security interest in collateral which qualifies for priority over a conflicting security interest under G.S. 25-9-327, 25-9-328, 25-9-329, 25-9-330, or 25-9-331 also has priority over a conflicting security interest in:

(1) Any supporting obligation for the collateral; and

(2) Proceeds of the collateral if:

a. The security interest in proceeds is perfected;

b. The proceeds are cash proceeds or of the same type as the collateral; and

c. In the case of proceeds that are proceeds of proceeds, all intervening proceeds are cash proceeds, proceeds of the same type as the collateral, or an account relating to the collateral.

(d) First-to-file priority rule for certain collateral. - Subject to subsection (e) of this section and except as otherwise provided in subsection (f) of this section, if a security interest in chattel paper, deposit accounts, negotiable documents, instruments, investment property, or letter-of-credit rights is perfected by a method other than filing, conflicting perfected security interests in proceeds of the collateral rank according to priority in time of filing.

(e) Applicability of subsection (d). - Subsection (d) of this section applies only if the proceeds of the collateral are not cash proceeds, chattel paper, negotiable documents, instruments, investment property, or letter-of-credit rights.

(f) Limitations on subsections (a) through (e). - Subsections (a) through (e) of this section are subject to:

(1) Subsection (g) of this section and the other provisions of this Part;

(2) G.S. 25-4-208 with respect to a security interest of a collecting bank;

(3) G.S. 25-5-118 with respect to a security interest of an issuer or nominated person; and

(4) G.S. 25-9-110 with respect to a security interest arising under Article 2 or 2A of this Chapter.

(g) Priority under agricultural lien statute. - A perfected agricultural lien on collateral has priority over a conflicting security interest in or agricultural lien on the same collateral if the statute creating the agricultural lien so provides. (1866-7, c. 1, s. 1; 1872-3, c. 133, s. 1; Code, s. 1799; 1893, c. 9; Rev., s. 2052; C.S., s. 2480; 1925, c. 302, s. 1; 1927, c. 22; 1935, c. 205; 1945, c. 196, s. 4; 1955, c. 816; 1957, c. 999; 1965, c. 700, s. 1; 1967, c. 24, s. 13; 1975, c. 862, s. 7; 1979, c. 404, s. 2; 1989 (Reg. Sess., 1990), c. 1024, s. 8(o); 1997-181, ss. 15, 16; 1997-336, s. 1; 1997-456, s. 5; 2000-169, s. 1.)

§ 25-9-323. Future advances.

(a) When priority based on time of advance. - Except as otherwise provided in subsection (c) of this section, for purposes of determining the priority of a perfected security interest under G.S. 25-9-322(a)(1), perfection of the security interest dates from the time an advance is made to the extent that the security interest secures an advance that:

(1) Is made while the security interest is perfected only:

a. Under G.S. 25-9-309 when it attaches; or

b. Temporarily under G.S. 25-9-312(e), (f), or (g); and

(2) Is not made pursuant to a commitment entered into before or while the security interest is perfected by a method other than under G.S. 25-9-309 or G.S. 25-9-312(e), (f), or (g).

(b)   Lien creditor. - Except as otherwise provided in subsection (c) of this section, a security interest is subordinate to the rights of a person that becomes a lien creditor to the extent that the security interest secures an advance made more than 45 days after the person becomes a lien creditor unless the advance is made:

(1)   Without knowledge of the lien; or

(2)   Pursuant to a commitment entered into without knowledge of the lien.

(c)   Buyer of receivables. - Subsections (a) and (b) of this section do not apply to a security interest held by a secured party that is a buyer of accounts, chattel paper, payment intangibles, or promissory notes or a consignor.

(d)   Buyer of goods. - Except as otherwise provided in subsection (e) of this section, a buyer of goods other than a buyer in ordinary course of business takes free of a security interest to the extent that it secures advances made after the earlier of:

(1)   The time the secured party acquires knowledge of the buyer's purchase; or

(2)   45 days after the purchase.

(e)   Advances made pursuant to commitment: priority of buyer of goods. - Subsection (d) of this section does not apply if the advance is made pursuant to a commitment entered into without knowledge of the buyer's purchase and before the expiration of the 45-day period.

(f)   Lessee of goods. - Except as otherwise provided in subsection (g) of this section, a lessee of goods, other than a lessee in ordinary course of business, takes the leasehold interest free of a security interest to the extent that it secures advances made after the earlier of:

(1)   The time the secured party acquires knowledge of the lease; or

(2)   45 days after the lease contract becomes enforceable.

(g)   Advances made pursuant to commitment: priority of lessee of goods. - Subsection (f) of this section does not apply if the advance is made pursuant to a commitment entered into without knowledge of the lease and before the expiration of the 45-day period. (1945, c. 182, s. 4; c. 196, s. 4; 1955, c. 386, s. 2; 1961, c. 574; 1965, c. 700, s. 1; 1975, c. 862, s. 7; 1979, c. 404, s. 1; 1997-181, s. 8; 2000-169, s. 1.)

§ 25-9-324. Priority of purchase-money security interests.

(a) General rule: purchase-money priority. - Except as otherwise provided in subsection (g) of this section, a perfected purchase-money security interest in goods other than inventory or livestock has priority over a conflicting security interest in the same goods, and, except as otherwise provided in G.S. 25-9-327, a perfected security interest in its identifiable proceeds also has priority, if the purchase-money security interest is perfected when the debtor receives possession of the collateral or within 20 days thereafter.

(b) Inventory purchase-money priority. - Subject to subsection (c) of this section and except as otherwise provided in subsection (g) of this section, a perfected purchase-money security interest in inventory has priority over a conflicting security interest in the same inventory, has priority over a conflicting security interest in chattel paper or an instrument constituting proceeds of the inventory and in proceeds of the chattel paper, if so provided in G.S. 25-9-330, and, except as otherwise provided in G.S. 25-9-327, also has priority in identifiable cash proceeds of the inventory to the extent the identifiable cash proceeds are received on or before the delivery of the inventory to a buyer, if:

(1) The purchase-money security interest is perfected when the debtor receives possession of the inventory;

(2) The purchase-money secured party sends an authenticated notification to the holder of the conflicting security interest;

(3) The holder of the conflicting security interest receives the notification within five years before the debtor receives possession of the inventory; and

(4) The notification states that the person sending the notification has or expects to acquire a purchase-money security interest in inventory of the debtor and describes the inventory.

(c) Holders of conflicting inventory security interests to be notified. - Subdivisions (b)(2) through (b)(4) of this section apply only if the holder of the conflicting security interest had filed a financing statement covering the same types of inventory:

(1) If the purchase-money security interest is perfected by filing, before the date of the filing; or

(2) If the purchase-money security interest is temporarily perfected without filing or possession under G.S. 25-9-312(f), before the beginning of the 20-day period thereunder.

(d) Livestock purchase-money priority. - Subject to subsection (e) of this section and except as otherwise provided in subsection (g) of this section, a perfected purchase-money security interest in livestock that are farm products has priority over a conflicting security interest in the same livestock, and, except as otherwise provided in G.S. 25-9-327, a perfected security interest in their identifiable proceeds and identifiable products in their unmanufactured states also has priority, if:

(1) The purchase-money security interest is perfected when the debtor receives possession of the livestock;

(2) The purchase-money secured party sends an authenticated notification to the holder of the conflicting security interest;

(3) The holder of the conflicting security interest receives the notification within six months before the debtor receives possession of the livestock; and

(4) The notification states that the person sending the notification has or expects to acquire a purchase-money security interest in livestock of the debtor and describes the livestock.

(e) Holders of conflicting livestock security interests to be notified. - Subdivisions (d)(2) through (d)(4) of this section apply only if the holder of the conflicting security interest had filed a financing statement covering the same types of livestock:

(1) If the purchase-money security interest is perfected by filing, before the date of the filing; or

(2) If the purchase-money security interest is temporarily perfected without filing or possession under G.S. 25-9-312(f), before the beginning of the 20-day period thereunder.

(f) Software purchase-money priority. - Except as otherwise provided in subsection (g) of this section, a perfected purchase-money security interest in software has priority over a conflicting security interest in the same collateral, and, except as otherwise provided in G.S. 25-9-327, a perfected security interest in its identifiable proceeds also has priority, to the extent that the purchase-money security interest in the goods in which the software was acquired for use has priority in the goods and proceeds of the goods under this section.

(g) Conflicting purchase-money security interests. - If more than one security interest qualifies for priority in the same collateral under subsection (a), (b), (d), or (f) of this section:

(1) A security interest securing an obligation incurred as all or part of the price of the collateral has priority over a security interest securing an obligation incurred for value given to enable the debtor to acquire rights in or the use of collateral; and

(2) In all other cases, G.S. 25-9-322(a) applies to the qualifying security interests. (1945, c. 182, s. 4; c. 196, s. 4; 1955, c. 386, s. 2; 1961, c. 574; 1965, c. 700, s. 1; 1975, c. 862, s. 7; 1979, c. 404, s. 1; 1997-181, s. 8; 2000-169, s. 1.)

§ 25-9-324.1. Priority of production-money security interests and agricultural liens.

(a) Priority over conflicting security interests. - Except as otherwise provided in subsections (c), (d), and (e) of this section, if the requirements of subsection (b) of this section are satisfied, a perfected production-money security interest in production-money crops has priority over a conflicting security interest in the same crops and, except as otherwise provided in G.S. 25-9-327, also has priority in their identifiable proceeds.

(b) Requirements for priority. - A production-money security interest has priority under subsection (a) of this section if:

(1) The production-money security interest is perfected by filing when the production-money secured party first gives new value to enable the debtor to produce the crops;

(2) The production-money secured party sends an authenticated notification to the holder of the conflicting security interest not less than 10 or more than 30 days before the production-money secured party first gives new value to enable the debtor to produce the crops if the holder had filed a financing statement covering the crops before the date of the filing made by the production-money secured party; and

(3) The notification states that the production-money secured party has or expects to acquire a production-money security interest in the debtor's crops and provides a description of the crops.

(c) Multiple production-money security interests. - Except as otherwise provided in subsection (d) or (e) of this section, if more than one security interest qualifies for priority in the same collateral under subsection (a) of this section, the security interests rank according to priority in time of filing under G.S. 25-9-322(a).

(d) New value to produce production-money crops. - To the extent that a person holding a perfected security interest in production-money crops that are the subject of a production-money security interest gives new value to enable the debtor to produce the production-money crops and the value is in fact used for the production of the production-money crops, the security interests rank according to priority in time of filing under G.S. 25-9-322(a).

(e) Holder of agricultural lien and production-money security interest. - To the extent that a person holds both an agricultural lien and a production-money security interest in the same collateral securing the same obligations, the rules of priority applicable to agricultural liens govern priority.

(f) Creating or perfecting production-money security interest not to operate as default or accelerating event. - Creating or perfecting a production-money security interest shall not operate under any circumstances as a default on, an accelerating event under, or otherwise as a breach of any note or other instrument or agreement of any kind or nature to pay debt, any loan or credit agreement, or any security agreement or arrangement of any kind or nature where the collateral is real or personal property. (1866-7, c. 1, s. 1; 1872-3, c.

133, s. 1; Code, s. 1799; 1893, c. 9; Rev., s. 2052; C.S., s. 2480; 1925, c. 302, s. 1; 1927, c. 22; 1935, c. 205; 1945, c. 196, s. 4; 1955, c. 816; 1957, c. 999; 1965, c. 700, s. 1; 1967, c. 24, s. 13; 1975, c. 862, s. 7; 1979, c. 404, s. 2; 1989 (Reg. Sess., 1990), c. 1024, s. 8(o); 1997-181, ss. 15, 16; 1997-336, s. 1; 1997-456, s. 5; 2000-169, s. 1.)

§ 25-9-325. Priority of security interests in transferred collateral.

(a) Subordination of security interest in transferred collateral. - Except as otherwise provided in subsection (b) of this section, a security interest created by a debtor is subordinate to a security interest in the same collateral created by another person if:

(1) The debtor acquired the collateral subject to the security interest created by the other person;

(2) The security interest created by the other person was perfected when the debtor acquired the collateral; and

(3) There is no period thereafter when the security interest is unperfected.

(b) Limitation of subsection (a) subordination. - Subsection (a) of this section subordinates a security interest only if the security interest:

(1) Otherwise would have priority solely under G.S. 25-9-322(a) or G.S. 25-9-324; or

(2) Arose solely under G.S. 25-2-711(3) or G.S. 25-2A-508(5). (2000-169, s. 1.)

§ 25-9-326. Priority of security interests created by new debtor.

(a) Subordination of security interest created by new debtor. - Subject to subsection (b) of this section, a security interest that is created by a new debtor in collateral in which the new debtor has or acquires rights and is perfected solely by a filed financing statement that would be ineffective to perfect the security interest but for the application of G.S. 25-9-316(i)(1) or G.S. 25-9-508 is subordinate to a security interest in the same collateral which is perfected other than by such a filed financing statement.

(b) Priority under other provisions; multiple original debtors. - The other provisions of this Part determine the priority among conflicting security interests in the same collateral perfected by filed financing statements described in subsection (a) of this section. However, if the security agreements to which a new debtor became bound as debtor were not entered into by the same original debtor, the conflicting security interests rank according to priority in time of the new debtor's having become bound. (2000-169, s. 1; 2012-70, s. 7.)

§ 25-9-327. Priority of security interests in deposit account.

The following rules govern priority among conflicting security interests in the same deposit account:

(1) A security interest held by a secured party having control of the deposit account under G.S. 25-9-104 has priority over a conflicting security interest held by a secured party that does not have control.

(2) Except as otherwise provided in subdivisions (3) and (4) of this section, security interests perfected by control under G.S. 25-9-314 rank according to priority in time of obtaining control.

(3) Except as otherwise provided in subdivision (4) of this section, a security interest held by the bank with which the deposit account is maintained has priority over a conflicting security interest held by another secured party.

(4) A security interest perfected by control under G.S. 25-9-104(a)(3) has priority over a security interest held by the bank with which the deposit account is maintained. (1997-181, s. 5; 2000-169, s. 1.)

§ 25-9-328. Priority of security interests in investment property.

The following rules govern priority among conflicting security interests in the same investment property:

(1) A security interest held by a secured party having control of investment property under G.S. 25-9-106 has priority over a security interest held by a secured party that does not have control of the investment property.

(2) Except as otherwise provided in subdivisions (3) and (4) of this section, conflicting security interests held by secured parties each of which has control under G.S. 25-9-106 rank according to priority in time of:

a. If the collateral is a security, obtaining control;

b. If the collateral is a security entitlement carried in a securities account and:

1. If the secured party obtained control under G.S. 25-8-106(d)(1), the secured party's becoming the person for which the securities account is maintained;

2. If the secured party obtained control under G.S. 25-8-106(d)(2), the securities intermediary's agreement to comply with the secured party's entitlement orders with respect to security entitlements carried or to be carried in the securities account; or

3. If the secured party obtained control through another person under G.S. 25-8-106(d)(3), the time on which priority would be based under this subdivision if the other person were the secured party; or

c. If the collateral is a commodity contract carried with a commodity intermediary, the satisfaction of the requirement for control specified in G.S. 25-9-106(b)(2) with respect to commodity contracts carried or to be carried with the commodity intermediary.

(3) A security interest held by a securities intermediary in a security entitlement or a securities account maintained with the securities intermediary has priority over a conflicting security interest held by another secured party.

(4) A security interest held by a commodity intermediary in a commodity contract or a commodity account maintained with the commodity intermediary has priority over a conflicting security interest held by another secured party.

(5) A security interest in a certificated security in registered form which is perfected by taking delivery under G.S. 25-9-313(a) and not by control under

G.S. 25-9-314 has priority over a conflicting security interest perfected by a method other than control.

(6) Conflicting security interests created by a broker, securities intermediary, or commodity intermediary which are perfected without control under G.S. 25-9-106 rank equally.

(7) In all other cases, priority among conflicting security interests in investment property is governed by G.S. 25-9-322 and G.S. 25-9-323. (1997-181, s. 5; 2000-169, s. 1.)

§ 25-9-329. Priority of security interests in letter-of-credit right.

The following rules govern priority among conflicting security interests in the same letter-of-credit right:

(1) A security interest held by a secured party having control of the letter-of-credit right under G.S. 25-9-107 has priority to the extent of its control over a conflicting security interest held by a secured party that does not have control.

(2) Security interests perfected by control under G.S. 25-9-314 rank according to priority in time of obtaining control. (1997-181, s. 5; 2000-169, s. 1.)

§ 25-9-330. Priority of purchaser of chattel paper or instrument.

(a) Purchaser's priority: security interest claimed merely as proceeds. - A purchaser of chattel paper has priority over a security interest in the chattel paper which is claimed merely as proceeds of inventory subject to a security interest if:

(1) In good faith and in the ordinary course of the purchaser's business, the purchaser gives new value and takes possession of the chattel paper or obtains control of the chattel paper under G.S. 25-9-105; and

(2) The chattel paper does not indicate that it has been assigned to an identified assignee other than the purchaser.

(b)   Purchaser's priority: other security interests. - A purchaser of chattel paper has priority over a security interest in the chattel paper which is claimed other than merely as proceeds of inventory subject to a security interest if the purchaser gives new value and takes possession of the chattel paper or obtains control of the chattel paper under G.S. 25-9-105 in good faith, in the ordinary course of the purchaser's business, and without knowledge that the purchase violates the rights of the secured party.

(c)   Chattel paper purchaser's priority in proceeds. - Except as otherwise provided in G.S. 25-9-327, a purchaser having priority in chattel paper under subsection (a) or (b) of this section also has priority in proceeds of the chattel paper to the extent that:

(1)   G.S. 25-9-322 provides for priority in the proceeds; or

(2)   The proceeds consist of the specific goods covered by the chattel paper or cash proceeds of the specific goods, even if the purchaser's security interest in the proceeds is unperfected.

(d)   Instrument purchaser's priority. - Except as otherwise provided in G.S. 25-9-331(a), a purchaser of an instrument has priority over a security interest in the instrument perfected by a method other than possession if the purchaser gives value and takes possession of the instrument in good faith and without knowledge that the purchase violates the rights of the secured party.

(e)   Holder of purchase-money security interest gives new value. - For purposes of subsections (a) and (b) of this section, the holder of a purchase-money security interest in inventory gives new value for chattel paper constituting proceeds of the inventory.

(f)   Indication of assignment gives knowledge. - For purposes of subsections (b) and (d) of this section, if chattel paper or an instrument indicates that it has been assigned to an identified secured party other than the purchaser, a purchaser of the chattel paper or instrument has knowledge that the purchase violates the rights of the secured party. (1961, c. 574; 1965, c. 700, s. 1; 1975, c. 862, s. 7; 2000-169, s. 1.)

§ 25-9-331. Priority of rights of purchasers of instruments, documents, and securities under other Articles; priority of interests in financial assets and security entitlements under Article 8.

(a) Rights under Articles 3, 7, and 8 not limited. - This Article does not limit the rights of a holder in due course of a negotiable instrument, a holder to which a negotiable document of title has been duly negotiated, or a protected purchaser of a security. These holders or purchasers take priority over an earlier security interest, even if perfected, to the extent provided in Articles 3, 7, and 8 of this Chapter.

(b) Protection under Article 8. - This Article does not limit the rights of or impose liability on a person to the extent that the person is protected against the assertion of a claim under Article 8 of this Chapter.

(c) Filing not notice. - Filing under this Article does not constitute notice of a claim or defense to the holders, or purchasers, or persons described in subsections (a) and (b) of this section. (1961, c. 574; 1965, c. 700, s. 1; 1975, c. 862, s. 7; 1989 (Reg. Sess., 1990), c. 1024, s. 8(m), (n); 1997-181, s. 14; 2000-169, s. 1.)

§ 25-9-332. Transfer of money; transfer of funds from deposit account.

(a) Transferee of money. - A transferee of money takes the money free of a security interest unless the transferee acts in collusion with the debtor in violating the rights of the secured party.

(b) Transferee of funds from deposit account. - A transferee of funds from a deposit account takes the funds free of a security interest in the deposit account unless the transferee acts in collusion with the debtor in violating the rights of the secured party. (2000-169, s. 1.)

§ 25-9-333. Priority of certain liens arising by operation of law.

(a) "Possessory lien." - In this section, "possessory lien" means an interest, other than a security interest or an agricultural lien:

(1) Which secures payment or performance of an obligation for services or materials furnished with respect to goods by a person in the ordinary course of the person's business;

(2) Which is created by statute or rule of law in favor of the person; and

(3) Whose effectiveness depends on the person's possession of the goods.

(b) Priority of possessory lien. - A possessory lien on goods has priority over a security interest in the goods unless the lien is created by a statute that expressly provides otherwise. (1965, c. 700, s. 1; 1975, c. 862, s. 7; 2000-169, s. 1.)

§ 25-9-334. Priority of security interests in fixtures and crops.

(a) Security interest in fixtures under this Article. - A security interest under this Article may be created in goods that are fixtures or may continue in goods that become fixtures. A security interest does not exist under this Article in ordinary building materials incorporated into an improvement on land.

(b) Security interest in fixtures under real-property law. - This Article does not prevent creation of an encumbrance upon fixtures under real property law.

(c) General rule: subordination of security interest in fixtures. - In cases not governed by subsections (d) through (h) of this section, a security interest in fixtures is subordinate to a conflicting interest of an encumbrancer or owner of the related real property other than the debtor.

(d) Fixtures purchase-money priority. - Except as otherwise provided in subsection (h) of this section, a perfected security interest in fixtures has priority over a conflicting interest of an encumbrancer or owner of the real property if the debtor has an interest of record in or is in possession of the real property and:

(1) The security interest is a purchase-money security interest;

(2) The interest of the encumbrancer or owner arises before the goods become fixtures; and

(3) The security interest is perfected by a fixture filing before the goods become fixtures or within 20 days thereafter.

(e) Priority of security interest in fixtures over interests in real property. - A perfected security interest in fixtures has priority over a conflicting interest of an encumbrancer or owner of the real property if:

(1) The debtor has an interest of record in the real property or is in possession of the real property and the security interest:

a. Is perfected by a fixture filing before the interest of the encumbrancer or owner is of record; and

b. Has priority over any conflicting interest of a predecessor in title of the encumbrancer or owner;

(2) Before the goods become fixtures, the security interest is perfected by any method permitted by this Article and the fixtures are readily removable:

a. Factory or office machines;

b. Equipment that is not primarily used or leased for use in the operation of the real property; or

c. Replacements of domestic appliances that are consumer goods;

(3) The conflicting interest is a lien on the real property obtained by legal or equitable proceedings after the security interest was perfected by any method permitted by this Article; or

(4) The security interest is:

a. Created in a manufactured home in a manufactured-home transaction; and

b. Perfected pursuant to a statute described in G.S. 25-9-311(a)(2).

(f) Priority based on consent, disclaimer, or right to remove. - A security interest in fixtures, whether or not perfected, has priority over a conflicting interest of an encumbrancer or owner of the real property if:

(1)   The encumbrancer or owner has, in an authenticated record, consented to the security interest or disclaimed an interest in the goods as fixtures; or

(2)   The debtor has a right to remove the goods as against the encumbrancer or owner.

(g)   Continuation of subdivision (f)(2) priority. - The priority of the security interest under subdivision (f)(2) of this section continues for a reasonable time if the debtor's right to remove the goods as against the encumbrancer or owner terminates.

(h)   Priority of construction mortgage. - A mortgage is a construction mortgage to the extent that it secures an obligation incurred for the construction of an improvement on land, including the acquisition cost of the land, if a recorded record of the mortgage so indicates. Except as otherwise provided in subsections (e) and (f) of this section, a security interest in fixtures is subordinate to a construction mortgage if a record of the mortgage is recorded before the goods become fixtures and the goods become fixtures before the completion of the construction. A mortgage has this priority to the same extent as a construction mortgage to the extent that it is given to refinance a construction mortgage.

(i)   Priority of security interest in crops. - Except as provided in G.S. 42-15, a perfected security interest in crops growing on real property has priority over a conflicting interest of an encumbrancer or owner of the real property if the debtor has an interest of record in or is in possession of the real property. (1965, c. 700, s. 1; 1967, c. 562, s. 1; 1975, c. 862, s. 7; 2000-169, s. 1.)

§ 25-9-335. Accessions.

(a)   Creation of security interest in accession. - A security interest may be created in an accession and continues in collateral that becomes an accession.

(b)   Perfection of security interest. - If a security interest is perfected when the collateral becomes an accession, the security interest remains perfected in the collateral.

(c) Priority of security interest. - Except as otherwise provided in subsection (d) of this section, the other provisions of this Part determine the priority of a security interest in an accession.

(d) Compliance with certificate-of-title statute. - A security interest in an accession is subordinate to a security interest in the whole which is perfected by compliance with the requirements of a certificate-of-title statute under G.S. 25-9-311(b).

(e) Removal of accession after default. - After default, subject to Part 6 of this Article, a secured party may remove an accession from other goods if the security interest in the accession has priority over the claims of every person having an interest in the whole.

(f) Reimbursement following removal. - A secured party that removes an accession from other goods under subsection (e) of this section shall promptly reimburse any holder of a security interest or other lien on, or owner of, the whole or of the other goods, other than the debtor, for the cost of repair of any physical injury to the whole or the other goods. The secured party need not reimburse the holder or owner for any diminution in value of the whole or the other goods caused by the absence of the accession removed or by any necessity for replacing it. A person entitled to reimbursement may refuse permission to remove until the secured party gives adequate assurance for the performance of the obligation to reimburse. (1965, c. 700, s. 1; 1975, c. 862, s. 7; 2000-169, s. 1.)

§ 25-9-336. Commingled goods.

(a) "Commingled goods." - In this section, "commingled goods" means goods that are physically united with other goods in such a manner that their identity is lost in a product or mass.

(b) No security interest in commingled goods as such. - A security interest does not exist in commingled goods as such. However, a security interest may attach to a product or mass that results when goods become commingled goods.

(c) Attachment of security interest to product or mass. - If collateral becomes commingled goods, a security interest attaches to the product or mass.

(d) Perfection of security interest. - If a security interest in collateral is perfected before the collateral becomes commingled goods, the security interest that attaches to the product or mass under subsection (c) of this section is perfected.

(e) Priority of security interest. - Except as otherwise provided in subsection (f) of this section, the other provisions of this Part determine the priority of a security interest that attaches to the product or mass under subsection (c) of this section.

(f) Conflicting security interests in product or mass. - If more than one security interest attaches to the product or mass under subsection (c) of this section, the following rules determine priority:

(1) A security interest that is perfected under subsection (d) of this section has priority over a security interest that is unperfected at the time the collateral becomes commingled goods.

(2) If more than one security interest is perfected under subsection (d) of this section, the security interests rank equally in proportion to the value of the collateral at the time it became commingled goods. (1965, c. 700, s. 1; 1975, c. 862, s. 7; 2000-169, s. 1.)

§ 25-9-337. Priority of security interests in goods covered by certificate of title.

If, while a security interest in goods is perfected by any method under the law of another jurisdiction, this State issues a certificate of title that does not show that the goods are subject to the security interest or contain a statement that they may be subject to security interests not shown on the certificate:

(1) A buyer of the goods, other than a person in the business of selling goods of that kind, takes free of the security interest if the buyer gives value and receives delivery of the goods after issuance of the certificate and without knowledge of the security interest; and

(2) The security interest is subordinate to a conflicting security interest in the goods that attaches, and is perfected under G.S. 25-9-311(b), after issuance of the certificate and without the conflicting secured party's knowledge of the security interest. (1945, c. 196, s. 2; 1957, c. 564; 1965, c. 700, s. 1; 1967, c. 562, s. 1; 1975, c. 862, s. 7; 1989 (Reg. Sess., 1990), c. 1024, s. 8(e), (f); 1997-181, s. 2; 1999-73, s. 4(a), (b); 2000-169, s. 1.)

§ 25-9-338. Priority of security interest or agricultural lien perfected by filed financing statement providing certain incorrect information.

If a security interest or agricultural lien is perfected by a filed financing statement providing information described in G.S. 25-9-516(b)(5) which is incorrect at the time the financing statement is filed:

(1) The security interest or agricultural lien is subordinate to a conflicting perfected security interest in the collateral to the extent that the holder of the conflicting security interest gives value in reasonable reliance upon the incorrect information; and

(2) A purchaser, other than a secured party, of the collateral takes free of the security interest or agricultural lien to the extent that, in reasonable reliance upon the incorrect information, the purchaser gives value and, in the case of tangible chattel paper, tangible documents, goods, instruments, or a security certificate, receives delivery of the collateral. (2000-169, s. 1; 2006-112, s. 54.)

§ 25-9-339. Priority subject to subordination.

This Article does not preclude subordination by agreement by a person entitled to priority. (1965, c. 700, s. 1; 1975, c. 862, s. 7; 2000-169, s. 1.)

SUBPART 4. Rights of Banks.

§ 25-9-340. Effectiveness of right of recoupment or setoff against deposit account.

(a) Exercise of recoupment or setoff. - Except as otherwise provided in subsection (c) of this section, a bank with which a deposit account is maintained may exercise any right of recoupment or setoff against a secured party that holds a security interest in the deposit account.

(b) Recoupment or setoff not affected by security interest. - Except as otherwise provided in subsection (c) of this section, the application of this Article to a security interest in a deposit account does not affect a right of recoupment or setoff of the secured party as to a deposit account maintained with the secured party.

(c) When setoff ineffective. - The exercise by a bank of a setoff against a deposit account is ineffective against a secured party that holds a security interest in the deposit account which is perfected by control under G.S. 25-9-104(a)(3), if the setoff is based on a claim against the debtor. (2000-169, s. 1.)

§ 25-9-341. Bank's rights and duties with respect to deposit account.

Except as otherwise provided in G.S. 25-9-340(c), and unless the bank otherwise agrees in an authenticated record, a bank's rights and duties with respect to a deposit account maintained with the bank are not terminated, suspended, or modified by:

(1) The creation, attachment, or perfection of a security interest in the deposit account;

(2) The bank's knowledge of the security interest; or

(3) The bank's receipt of instructions from the secured party. (2000-169, s. 1.)

§ 25-9-342. Bank's right to refuse to enter into or disclose existence of control agreement.

This Article does not require a bank to enter into an agreement of the kind described in G.S. 25-9-104(a)(2), even if its customer so requests or directs. A bank that has entered into such an agreement is not required to confirm the existence of the agreement to another person unless requested to do so by its customer. (2000-169, s. 1.)

Part 4.

RIGHTS OF THIRD PARTIES.

§ 25-9-401. Alienability of debtor's rights.

(a) Other law governs alienability; exceptions. - Except as otherwise provided in subsection (b) of this section and G.S. 25-9-406, 25-9-407, 25-9-408, and 25-9-409, whether a debtor's rights in collateral may be voluntarily or involuntarily transferred is governed by law other than this Article.

(b) Agreement does not prevent transfer. - An agreement between the debtor and secured party which prohibits a transfer of the debtor's rights in collateral or makes the transfer a default does not prevent the transfer from taking effect. (1965, c. 700, s. 1; 1975, c. 862, s. 7; 2000-169, s. 1.)

§ 25-9-402. Secured party not obligated on contract of debtor or in tort.

The existence of a security interest, agricultural lien, or authority given to a debtor to dispose of or use collateral, without more, does not subject a secured party to liability in contract or tort for the debtor's acts or omissions. (1961, c. 574; 1965, c. 700, s. 1; 1975, c. 862, s. 7; 2000-169, s. 1.)

§ 25-9-403. Agreement not to assert defenses against assignee.

(a) "Value." - In this section, "value" has the meaning provided in G.S. 25-3-303(a).

(b) Agreement not to assert claim or defense. - Except as otherwise provided in this section, an agreement between an account debtor and an assignor not to assert against an assignee any claim or defense that the account debtor may have against the assignor is enforceable by an assignee that takes an assignment:

(1)   For value;

(2)   In good faith;

(3)   Without notice of a claim of a property or possessory right to the property assigned; and

(4)   Without notice of a defense or claim in recoupment of the type that may be asserted against a person entitled to enforce a negotiable instrument under G.S. 25-3-305(a).

(c)   When subsection (b) not applicable. - Subsection (b) of this section does not apply to defenses of a type that may be asserted against a holder in due course of a negotiable instrument under G.S. 25-3-305(b).

(d)   Omission of required statement in consumer transaction. - In a consumer transaction, if a record evidences the account debtor's obligation, law other than this Article requires that the record include a statement to the effect that the rights of an assignee are subject to claims or defenses that the account debtor could assert against the original obligee, and the record does not include such a statement:

(1)   The record has the same effect as if the record included such a statement; and

(2)   The account debtor may assert against an assignee those claims and defenses that would have been available if the record included such a statement.

(e)   Rule for individual under other law. - This section is subject to law other than this Article which establishes a different rule for an account debtor who is an individual and who incurred the obligation primarily for personal, family, or household purposes.

(f)   Other law not displaced. - Except as otherwise provided in subsection (d) of this section, this section does not displace law other than this Article which gives effect to an agreement by an account debtor not to assert a claim or defense against an assignee. (1965, c. 700, s. 1; 1975, c. 862, s. 7; 2000-169, s. 1.)

§ 25-9-404. Rights acquired by assignee; claims and defenses against assignee.

(a) Assignee's rights subject to terms, claims, and defenses; exceptions. - Unless an account debtor has made an enforceable agreement not to assert defenses or claims, and subject to subsections (b) through (e) of this section, the rights of an assignee are subject to:

(1) All terms of the agreement between the account debtor and assignor and any defense or claim in recoupment arising from the transaction that gave rise to the contract; and

(2) Any other defense or claim of the account debtor against the assignor which accrues before the account debtor receives a notification of the assignment authenticated by the assignor or the assignee.

(b) Account debtor's claim reduces amount owed to assignee. - Subject to subsection (c) of this section and except as otherwise provided in subsection (d) of this section, the claim of an account debtor against an assignor may be asserted against an assignee under subsection (a) of this section only to reduce the amount the account debtor owes.

(c) Rule for individual under other law. - This section is subject to law other than this Article which establishes a different rule for an account debtor who is an individual and who incurred the obligation primarily for personal, family, or household purposes.

(d) Omission of required statement in consumer transaction. - In a consumer transaction, if a record evidences the account debtor's obligation, law other than this Article requires that the record include a statement to the effect that the account debtor's recovery against an assignee with respect to claims and defenses against the assignor may not exceed amounts paid by the account debtor under the record, and the record does not include such a statement, the extent to which a claim of an account debtor against the assignor may be asserted against an assignee is determined as if the record included such a statement.

(e) Inapplicability to health-care-insurance receivable. - This section does not apply to an assignment of a health-care-insurance receivable. (1945, c. 196, s. 6; 1961, c. 574; 1965, c. 700, s. 1; 1975, c. 862, s. 7; 2000-169, s. 1.)

§ 25-9-405. Modification of assigned contract.

(a) Effect of modification on assignee. - A modification of or substitution for an assigned contract is effective against an assignee if made in good faith. The assignee acquires corresponding rights under the modified or substituted contract. The assignment may provide that the modification or substitution is a breach of contract by the assignor. This subsection is subject to subsections (b) through (d) of this section.

(b) Applicability of subsection (a). - Subsection (a) of this section applies to the extent that:

(1) The right to payment or a part thereof under an assigned contract has not been fully earned by performance; or

(2) The right to payment or a part thereof has been fully earned by performance and the account debtor has not received notification of the assignment under G.S. 25-9-406(a).

(c) Rule for individual under other law. - This section is subject to law other than this Article which establishes a different rule for an account debtor who is an individual and who incurred the obligation primarily for personal, family, or household purposes.

(d) Inapplicability to health-care-insurance receivable. - This section does not apply to an assignment of a health-care-insurance receivable. (1945, c. 196, s. 6; 1961, c. 574; 1965, c. 700, s. 1; 1975, c. 862, s. 7; 2000-169, s. 1.)

§ 25-9-406. Discharge of account debtor; notification of assignment; identification and proof of assignment; restrictions on assignment of accounts, chattel paper, payment intangibles, and promissory notes ineffective.

(a) Discharge of account debtor; effect of notification. - Subject to subsections (b) through (i) of this section, an account debtor on an account, chattel paper, or a payment intangible may discharge its obligation by paying the assignor until, but not after, the account debtor receives a notification, authenticated by the assignor or the assignee, that the amount due or to become due has been assigned and that payment is to be made to the assignee. After receipt of the notification, the account debtor may discharge its obligation by paying the assignee and may not discharge the obligation by paying the assignor.

(b) When notification ineffective. - Subject to subsection (h) of this section, notification is ineffective under subsection (a) of this section:

(1) If it does not reasonably identify the rights assigned;

(2) To the extent that an agreement between an account debtor and a seller of a payment intangible limits the account debtor's duty to pay a person other than the seller and the limitation is effective under law other than this Article; or

(3) At the option of an account debtor, if the notification notifies the account debtor to make less than the full amount of any installment or other periodic payment to the assignee, even if:

a. Only a portion of the account, chattel paper, or payment intangible has been assigned to that assignee;

b. A portion has been assigned to another assignee; or

c. The account debtor knows that the assignment to that assignee is limited.

(c) Proof of assignment. - Subject to subsection (h) of this section, if requested by the account debtor, an assignee shall seasonably furnish reasonable proof that the assignment has been made. Unless the assignee complies, the account debtor may discharge its obligation by paying the assignor, even if the account debtor has received a notification under subsection (a) of this section.

(d) Term restricting assignment generally ineffective. - Except as otherwise provided in subsection (e) of this section and G.S. 25-2A-303 and G.S. 25-9-407, and subject to subsection (h) of this section, a term in an agreement between an account debtor and an assignor or in a promissory note is ineffective to the extent that it:

(1) Prohibits, restricts, or requires the consent of the account debtor or person obligated on the promissory note to the assignment or transfer of, or the creation, attachment, perfection, or enforcement of a security interest in, the account, chattel paper, payment intangible, or promissory note; or

(2) Provides that the assignment or transfer or the creation, attachment, perfection, or enforcement of the security interest may give rise to a default, breach, right of recoupment, claim, defense, termination, right of termination, or remedy under the account, chattel paper, payment intangible, or promissory note.

(e) Inapplicability of subsection (d) to certain sales. - Subsection (d) of this section does not apply to the sale of a payment intangible or promissory note, other than a sale pursuant to a disposition under G.S. 25-9-610 or an acceptance of collateral under G.S. 25-9-620.

(f) Legal restrictions on assignment generally ineffective. - Except as otherwise provided in G.S. 25-2A-303 and G.S. 25-9-407 and subject to subsections (h) and (i) of this section, a rule of law, statute, or regulation that prohibits, restricts, or requires the consent of a government, governmental body or official, or account debtor to the assignment or transfer of, or creation of a security interest in, an account or chattel paper is ineffective to the extent that the rule of law, statute, or regulation:

(1) Prohibits, restricts, or requires the consent of the government, governmental body or official, or account debtor to the assignment or transfer of, or the creation, attachment, perfection, or enforcement of a security interest in the account or chattel paper; or

(2) Provides that the assignment or transfer or the creation, attachment, perfection, or enforcement of the security interest may give rise to a default, breach, right of recoupment, claim, defense, termination, right of termination, or remedy under the account or chattel paper.

(g) Subdivision (b)(3) not waivable. - Subject to subsection (h) of this section, an account debtor may not waive or vary its option under subdivision (b)(3) of this section.

(h) Rule for individual under other law. - This section is subject to law other than this Article which establishes a different rule for an account debtor who is an individual and who incurred the obligation primarily for personal, family, or household purposes.

(i) Inapplicability. - This section does not apply to an assignment of a health-care-insurance receivable or an interest in a partnership or limited liability company. Subsection (f) of this section does not apply to an assignment or transfer of, or the creation, attachment, perfection, or enforcement of a security interest in, a right the transfer of which is prohibited or restricted by any of the following statutes to the extent that the statute is inconsistent with subsection (f) of this section:

(1) North Carolina Structured Settlement Act (Article 44B of Chapter 1 of the General Statutes).

(2) North Carolina Crime Victims Compensation Act (Chapter 15B of the General Statutes).

(3) North Carolina Consumer Finance Act (Article 15 of Chapter 53 of the General Statutes).

(4) North Carolina Firefighters' and Rescue Squad Workers' Pension Fund (Article 86 of Chapter 58 of the General Statutes).

(5) Employment Security Law (Chapter 96 of the General Statutes).

(6) North Carolina Workers' Compensation Fund Act (Article 1 of Chapter 97 of the General Statutes).

(7) Programs of Public Assistance (Article 2 of Chapter 108A of the General Statutes).

(8) North Carolina State Lottery Act (Chapter 18C of the General Statutes).

(j) Section prevails over inconsistent law. - Except to the extent otherwise provided in subsection (i) of this section, this section prevails over any inconsistent provision of an existing or future statute, rule, or regulation of this State unless the provision is contained in a statute of this State, refers expressly to this section, and states that the provision prevails over this section. (1945, c.

196, s. 6; 1961, c. 574; 1965, c. 700, s. 1; 1975, c. 862, s. 7; 2000-169, s. 1; 2012-70, s. 8; 2013-157, s. 31; 2013-284, s. 1(b).)

§ 25-9-407. Restrictions on creation or enforcement of security interest in leasehold interest or in lessor's residual interest.

(a) Term restricting assignment generally ineffective. - Except as otherwise provided in subsection (b) of this section, a term in a lease agreement is ineffective to the extent that it:

(1) Prohibits, restricts, or requires the consent of a party to the lease to the assignment or transfer of, or the creation, attachment, perfection, or enforcement of a security interest in, an interest of a party under the lease contract or in the lessor's residual interest in the goods; or

(2) Provides that the assignment or transfer or the creation, attachment, perfection, or enforcement of the security interest may give rise to a default, breach, right of recoupment, claim, defense, termination, right of termination, or remedy under the lease.

(b) Effectiveness of certain terms. - Except as otherwise provided in G.S. 25-2A-303(7), a term described in subdivision (a)(2) of this section is effective to the extent that there is:

(1) A transfer by the lessee of the lessee's right of possession or use of the goods in violation of the term; or

(2) A delegation of a material performance of either party to the lease contract in violation of the term.

(c) Security interest not material impairment. - The creation, attachment, perfection, or enforcement of a security interest in the lessor's interest under the lease contract or the lessor's residual interest in the goods is not a transfer that materially impairs the lessee's prospect of obtaining return performance or materially changes the duty of or materially increases the burden or risk imposed on the lessee within the purview of G.S. 25-2A-303(4) unless, and then only to the extent that, enforcement actually results in a delegation of material performance of the lessor. (1993, c. 463, s. 1; 2000-169, s. 1.)

§ 25-9-408. Restrictions on assignment of promissory notes, health-care-insurance receivables, and certain general intangibles ineffective.

(a) Term restricting assignment generally ineffective. - Except as otherwise provided in subsection (b) of this section, a term in a promissory note or in an agreement between an account debtor and a debtor which relates to a health-care-insurance receivable or a general intangible, including a contract, permit, license, or franchise, and which term prohibits, restricts, or requires the consent of the person obligated on the promissory note or the account debtor to, the assignment or transfer of, or creation, attachment, or perfection of a security interest in, the promissory note, health-care-insurance receivable, or general intangible, is ineffective to the extent that the term:

(1) Would impair the creation, attachment, or perfection of a security interest; or

(2) Provides that the assignment or transfer or the creation, attachment, or perfection of the security interest may give rise to a default, breach, right of recoupment, claim, defense, termination, right of termination, or remedy under the promissory note, health-care-insurance receivable, or general intangible.

(b) Applicability of subsection (a) to sales of certain rights to payment. - Subsection (a) of this section applies to a security interest in a payment intangible or promissory note only if the security interest arises out of a sale of the payment intangible or promissory note, other than a sale pursuant to a disposition under G.S. 25-9-610 or an acceptance of collateral under G.S. 25-9-620.

(c) Legal restrictions on assignment generally ineffective. - A rule of law, statute, or regulation that prohibits, restricts, or requires the consent of a government, governmental body or official, person obligated on a promissory note, or account debtor to the assignment or transfer of, or creation of a security interest in, a promissory note, health-care-insurance receivable, or general intangible, including a contract, permit, license, or franchise between an account debtor and a debtor, is ineffective to the extent that the rule of law, statute, or regulation:

(1) Would impair the creation, attachment, or perfection of a security interest; or

(2) Provides that the assignment or transfer or the creation, attachment, or perfection of the security interest may give rise to a default, breach, right of recoupment, claim, defense, termination, right of termination, or remedy under the promissory note, health-care-insurance receivable, or general intangible.

(d) Limitation on ineffectiveness under subsections (a) and (c). - To the extent that a term in a promissory note or in an agreement between an account debtor and a debtor which relates to a health-care-insurance receivable or general intangible or a rule of law, statute, or regulation described in subsection (c) of this section would be effective under law other than this Article but is ineffective under subsection (a) or (c) of this section, the creation, attachment, or perfection of a security interest in the promissory note, health-care-insurance receivable, or general intangible:

(1) Is not enforceable against the person obligated on the promissory note or the account debtor;

(2) Does not impose a duty or obligation on the person obligated on the promissory note or the account debtor;

(3) Does not require the person obligated on the promissory note or the account debtor to recognize the security interest, pay or render performance to the secured party, or accept payment or performance from the secured party;

(4) Does not entitle the secured party to use or assign the debtor's rights under the promissory note, health-care-insurance receivable, or general intangible, including any related information or materials furnished to the debtor in the transaction giving rise to the promissory note, health-care-insurance receivable, or general intangible;

(5) Does not entitle the secured party to use, assign, possess, or have access to any trade secrets or confidential information of the person obligated on the promissory note or the account debtor; and

(6) Does not entitle the secured party to enforce the security interest in the promissory note, health-care-insurance receivable, or general intangible.

(e) Section prevails over inconsistent law. - Except to the extent otherwise provided in subsection (f) of this section, this section prevails over any inconsistent provision of an existing or future statute, rule, or regulation of this

State unless the provision is contained in a statute of this State, refers expressly to this section, and states that the provision prevails over this section.

(f) Inapplicability. - This section does not apply to an assignment of an interest in a partnership or limited liability company. Subsection (c) of this section does not apply to an assignment or transfer of, or the creation, attachment, perfection, or enforcement of a security interest in, a right the transfer of which is prohibited or restricted by any of the following statutes to the extent that the statute is inconsistent with subsection (c) of this section:

(1) North Carolina Structured Settlement Act (Article 44B of Chapter 1 of the General Statutes).

(2) North Carolina Crime Victims Compensation Act (Chapter 15B of the General Statutes).

(3) North Carolina Consumer Finance Act (Article 15 of Chapter 53 of the General Statutes).

(4) North Carolina Firefighters' and Rescue Squad Workers' Pension Fund (Article 86 of Chapter 58 of the General Statutes).

(5) Employment Security Law (Chapter 96 of the General Statutes).

(6) North Carolina Workers' Compensation Fund Act (Article 1 of Chapter 97 of the General Statutes).

(7) Programs of Public Assistance (Article 2 of Chapter 108A of the General Statutes).

(8) North Carolina State Lottery Act (Chapter 18C of the General Statutes). (2000-169, s. 1; 2012-70, s. 9; 2013-157, s. 32; 2013-284, s. 1(c).)

§ 25-9-409. Restrictions on assignment of letter-of-credit rights ineffective.

(a) Term or law restricting assignment generally ineffective. - A term in a letter of credit or a rule of law, statute, regulation, custom, or practice applicable to the letter of credit which prohibits, restricts, or requires the consent of an applicant, issuer, or nominated person to a beneficiary's assignment of or creation of a security interest in a letter-of-credit right is ineffective to the extent that the term or rule of law, statute, regulation, custom, or practice:

(1) Would impair the creation, attachment, or perfection of a security interest in the letter-of-credit right; or

(2) Provides that the assignment or the creation, attachment, or perfection of the security interest may give rise to a default, breach, right of recoupment, claim, defense, termination, right of termination, or remedy under the letter-of-credit right.

(b) Limitation on ineffectiveness under subsection (a). - To the extent that a term in a letter of credit is ineffective under subsection (a) of this section but would be effective under law other than this Article or a custom or practice applicable to the letter of credit, to the transfer of a right to draw or otherwise demand performance under the letter of credit, or to the assignment of a right to proceeds of the letter of credit, the creation, attachment, or perfection of a security interest in the letter-of-credit right:

(1) Is not enforceable against the applicant, issuer, nominated person, or transferee beneficiary;

(2) Imposes no duties or obligations on the applicant, issuer, nominated person, or transferee beneficiary; and

(3) Does not require the applicant, issuer, nominated person, or transferee beneficiary to recognize the security interest, pay or render performance to the secured party, or accept payment or other performance from the secured party. (2000-169, s. 1.)

Part 5.

FILING.

SUBPART 1. Filing Office; Contents and Effectiveness of Financing Statement.

§ 25-9-501. Filing offices.

(a) Filing offices. - Except as otherwise provided in subsection (b) of this section, if the local law of this State governs perfection of a security interest or agricultural lien, the office in which to file a financing statement to perfect the security interest or agricultural lien is:

(1) The office designated for the filing or recording of a record of a mortgage on the related real property, if:

a. The collateral is as-extracted collateral or timber to be cut; or

b. The financing statement is filed as a fixture filing and the collateral is goods that are or are to become fixtures; or

(2) The office of the Secretary of State, in all other cases, including a case in which the collateral is goods that are or are to become fixtures and the financing statement is not filed as a fixture filing.

(b) Filing office for transmitting utilities. - The office in which to file a financing statement to perfect a security interest in collateral, including fixtures, of a transmitting utility is the office of the Secretary of State. The financing statement also constitutes a fixture filing as to the collateral indicated in the financing statement which is or is to become fixtures. (1866-7, c. 1, s. 1; 1872-3, c. 133, s. 1; Code, s. 1799; 1893, c. 9; Rev., s. 2052; C.S., s. 2480; 1925, c. 302, s. 1; 1927, c. 22; 1935, c. 205; 1945, c. 182, s. 3; c. 196, s. 2; 1955, c. 816; 1957, cc. 564, 999; 1961, c. 574; 1965, c. 700, s. 1; 1975, c. 862, s. 7; 1983 (Reg. Sess., 1984), c. 1116, ss. 41, 42; 1989, c. 523, s. 3; 2000-169, s. 1.)

§ 25-9-502. Contents of financing statement; record of mortgage as financing statement; time of filing financing statement.

(a) Sufficiency of financing statement. - Subject to subsection (b) of this section, a financing statement is sufficient only if it:

(1) Provides the name of the debtor;

(2) Provides the name of the secured party or a representative of the secured party; and

(3) Indicates the collateral covered by the financing statement.

(b) Real-property-related financing statements. - Except as otherwise provided in G.S. 25-9-501(b), to be sufficient, a financing statement that covers as-extracted collateral or timber to be cut, or which is filed as a fixture filing and covers goods that are or are to become fixtures, must satisfy subsection (a) of this section and also:

(1) Indicate that it covers this type of collateral;

(2) Indicate that it is to be filed in the real property records;

(3) Provide a description of the real property to which the collateral is related; and

(4) If the debtor does not have an interest of record in the real property, provide the name of a record owner.

(c) Record of mortgage as financing statement. - A record of a mortgage is effective, from the date of recording, as a financing statement filed as a fixture filing or as a financing statement covering as-extracted collateral or timber to be cut only if:

(1) The record indicates the goods or accounts that it covers;

(2) The goods are or are to become fixtures related to the real property described in the record or the collateral is related to the real property described in the record and is as-extracted collateral or timber to be cut;

(3) The record satisfies the requirements for a financing statement in this section, but:

a. The record need not indicate that it is to be filed in the real property records; and

b. The record sufficiently provides the name of a debtor who is an individual if it provides the individual name of the debtor or the surname and first personal name of the debtor, even if the debtor is an individual to whom G.S. 25-9-503(a)(4) applies; and

(4) The record is duly recorded.

(d) Filing before security agreement or attachment. - A financing statement may be filed before a security agreement is made or a security interest otherwise attaches. (1899, cc. 17, 247; 1901, cc. 329, 704; 1903, c. 489; 1905, cc. 226, 319; Rev., s. 2055; 1907, c. 843; 1909, c. 532; P.L. 1913, c. 49; C.S., s. 2490; 1925, c. 285, s. 1; 1931, c. 196; 1933, c. 101, s. 6; 1945, c. 182, s. 2; c. 196, s. 2; 1951, c. 926, s. 1; 1955, c. 386, s. 1; 1957, c. 564; 1961, c. 574; 1965, c. 700, s. 1; 1969, c. 1115, s. 1; 1975, c. 862, s. 7; 1983 (Reg. Sess., 1984), c. 1116, s. 43; 1989, c. 523, s. 7; 2000-169, s. 1; 2012-70, s. 10.)

§ 25-9-503. Name of debtor and secured party.

(a) Sufficiency of debtor's name. - A financing statement sufficiently provides the name of the debtor:

(1) Except as otherwise provided in subdivision (3) of this subsection, if the debtor is a registered organization or the collateral is held in a trust that is a registered organization, only if the financing statement provides the name that is stated to be the registered organization's name on the public organic record most recently filed with or issued or enacted by the registered organization's jurisdiction of organization which purports to state, amend, or restate the registered organization's name;

(2) Subject to subsection (f) of this section, if the collateral is being administered by the personal representative of a decedent, only if the financing statement provides, as the name of the debtor, the name of the decedent and, in a separate part of the financing statement, indicates that the collateral is being administered by a personal representative;

(3) If the collateral is held in a trust that is not a registered organization, only if the financing statement:

a. Provides, as the name of the debtor:

1. If the organic record of the trust specifies a name for the trust, the name specified; or

2. If the organic record of the trust does not specify a name for the trust, the name of the settlor or testator; and

b. In a separate part of the financing statement:

1. If the name is provided in accordance with sub-subdivision a.1. of this subdivision, indicates that the collateral is held in a trust; or

2. If the name is provided in accordance with sub-subdivision a.2. of this subdivision, provides additional information sufficient to distinguish the trust from other trusts having one or more of the same settlors or the same testator and indicates that the collateral is held in a trust, unless the additional information so indicates;

(4) Subject to subsection (g) of this section, if the debtor is an individual to whom this State has issued a drivers license or special identification card that has not expired, only if the financing statement provides the name of the individual which is indicated on the drivers license or special identification card;

(5) If the debtor is an individual to whom subdivision (a)(4) of this section does not apply, only if the financing statement provides the individual name of the debtor or the surname and first personal name of the debtor; and

(6) In other cases:

a. If the debtor has a name, only if the financing statement provides the organizational name of the debtor; and

b. If the debtor does not have a name, only if the financing statement provides the names of the partners, members, associates, or other persons comprising the debtor, in a manner that each name provided would be sufficient if the person named were the debtor.

(b) Additional debtor-related information. - A financing statement that provides the name of the debtor in accordance with subsection (a) of this section is not rendered ineffective by the absence of:

(1) A trade name or other name of the debtor; or

(2) Unless required under sub-subdivision (a)(6)b. of this section, names of partners, members, associates, or other persons comprising the debtor.

(c) Debtor's trade name insufficient. - A financing statement that provides only the debtor's trade name does not sufficiently provide the name of the debtor.

(d) Representative capacity. - Failure to indicate the representative capacity of a secured party or representative of a secured party does not affect the sufficiency of a financing statement.

(e) Multiple debtors and secured parties. - A financing statement may provide the name of more than one debtor and the name of more than one secured party.

(f) Name of Decedent. - The name of the decedent indicated on the order appointing the personal representative of the decedent issued by the court having jurisdiction over the collateral is sufficient as the "name of the decedent" under subdivision (a)(2) of this section.

(g) Multiple Drivers Licenses or Special Identification Cards. - If this State has issued to an individual more than one drivers license or special identification card of a kind described in subdivision (a)(4) of this section, the one that was issued most recently is the one to which subdivision (a)(4) of this section refers.

(h) Definition. - In this section, the "name of the settlor or testator" means:

(1) If the settlor is a registered organization, the name that is stated to be the settlor's name on the public organic record most recently filed with or issued or enacted by the settlor's jurisdiction of organization which purports to state, amend, or restate the settlor's name; or

(2) In other cases, the name of the settlor or testator indicated in the trust's organic record. (1899, cc. 17, 247; 1901, cc. 329, 704; 1903, c. 489; 1905, cc. 226, 319; Rev., s. 2055; 1907, c. 843; 1909, c. 532; P.L. 1913, c. 49; C.S., s. 2490; 1925, c. 285, s. 1; 1931, c. 196; 1933, c. 101, s. 6; 1945, c. 182, s. 2; c. 196, s. 2; 1951, c. 926, s. 1; 1955, c. 386, s. 1; 1957, c. 564; 1961, c. 574; 1965, c. 700, s. 1; 1969, c. 1115, s. 1; 1975, c. 862, s. 7; 1983 (Reg. Sess., 1984), c. 1116, s. 43; 1989, c. 523, s. 7; 2000-169, s. 1; 2012-70, s. 11.)

§ 25-9-504. Indication of collateral.

A financing statement sufficiently indicates the collateral that it covers if the financing statement provides:

(1) A description of the collateral pursuant to G.S. 25-9-108; or

(2) An indication that the financing statement covers all assets or all personal property. (1899, cc. 17, 247; 1901, cc. 329, 704; 1903, c. 489; 1905, cc. 226, 319; Rev., s. 2055; 1907, c. 843; 1909, c. 532; P.L. 1913, c. 49; C.S., s. 2490; 1925, c. 285, s. 1; 1931, c. 196; 1933, c. 101, s. 6; 1945, c. 182, s. 2; c. 196, s. 2; 1951, c. 926, s. 1; 1955, c. 386, s. 1; 1957, c. 564; 1961, c. 574; 1965, c. 700, s. 1; 1969, c. 1115, s. 1; 1975, c. 862, s. 7; 1983 (Reg. Sess., 1984), c. 1116, s. 43; 1989, c. 523, s. 7; 2000-169, s. 1.)

§ 25-9-504.1. Deleted.

§ 25-9-504.2. Deleted.

§ 25-9-505. Filing and compliance with other statutes and treaties for consignments, leases, other bailments, and other transactions.

(a) Use of terms other than "debtor" and "secured party." - A consignor, lessor, or other bailor of goods, a licensor, or a buyer of a payment intangible or promissory note may file a financing statement, or may comply with a statute or treaty described in G.S. 25-9-311(a), using the terms "consignor", "consignee", "lessor", "lessee", "bailor", "bailee", "licensor", "licensee", "owner", "registered owner", "buyer", "seller", or words of similar import, instead of the terms "secured party" and "debtor".

(b) Effect of financing statement under subsection (a). - This Part applies to the filing of a financing statement under subsection (a) of this section and, as appropriate, to compliance that is equivalent to filing a financing statement under G.S. 25-9-311(b), but the filing or compliance is not of itself a factor in determining whether the collateral secures an obligation. If it is determined for another reason that the collateral secures an obligation, a security interest held by the consignor, lessor, bailor, licensor, owner, or buyer which attaches to the collateral is perfected by the filing or compliance. (1975, c. 862, s. 7; 2000-169, s. 1.)

§ 25-9-506. Effect of errors or omissions.

(a) Minor errors and omissions. - A financing statement substantially satisfying the requirements of this Part is effective, even if it has minor errors or omissions, unless the errors or omissions make the financing statement seriously misleading.

(b) Financing statement seriously misleading. - Except as otherwise provided in subsection (c) of this section, a financing statement that fails sufficiently to provide the name of the debtor in accordance with G.S. 25-9-503(a) is seriously misleading.

(c) Financing statement not seriously misleading. - If a search of the records of the filing office under the debtor's correct name, using the filing office's standard search logic, if any, would disclose a financing statement that fails sufficiently to provide the name of the debtor in accordance with G.S. 25-9-503(a), the name provided does not make the financing statement seriously misleading.

(d) "Debtor's correct name." - For purposes of G.S. 25-9-508(b), the "debtor's correct name" in subsection (c) of this section means the correct name of the new debtor. (1899, cc. 17, 247; 1901, cc. 329, 704; 1903, c. 489; 1905, cc. 226, 319; Rev., s. 2055; 1907, c. 843; 1909, c. 532; P.L. 1913, c. 49; C.S., s. 2490; 1925, c. 285, s. 1; 1931, c. 196; 1933, c. 101, s. 6; 1945, c. 182, s. 2; c. 196, s. 2; 1951, c. 926, s. 1; 1955, c. 386, s. 1; 1957, c. 564; 1961, c. 574; 1965, c. 700, s. 1; 1969, c. 1115, s. 1; 1975, c. 862, s. 7; 1983 (Reg. Sess., 1984), c. 1116, s. 43; 1989, c. 523, s. 7; 2000-169, s. 1.)

§ 25-9-507. Effect of certain events on effectiveness of financing statement.

(a) Disposition. - A filed financing statement remains effective with respect to collateral that is sold, exchanged, leased, licensed, or otherwise disposed of and in which a security interest or agricultural lien continues, even if the secured party knows of or consents to the disposition.

(b) Information becoming seriously misleading. - Except as otherwise provided in subsection (c) of this section and G.S. 25-9-508, a financing statement is not rendered ineffective if, after the financing statement is filed, the information provided in the financing statement becomes seriously misleading under G.S. 25-9-506.

(c) Change in debtor's name. - If the name that a filed financing statement provides for a debtor becomes insufficient as the name of the debtor under G.S. 25-9-503(a) so that the financing statement becomes seriously misleading under G.S. 25-9-506:

(1) The financing statement is effective to perfect a security interest in collateral acquired by the debtor before, or within four months after, the filed financing statement becomes seriously misleading; and

(2) The financing statement is not effective to perfect a security interest in collateral acquired by the debtor more than four months after the filed financing statement becomes seriously misleading, unless an amendment to the financing statement which renders the financing statement not seriously misleading is filed within four months after the financing statement became seriously misleading. (1899, cc. 17, 247; 1901, cc. 329, 704; 1903, c. 489; 1905, cc. 226, 319; Rev., s. 2055; 1907, c. 843; 1909, c. 532; P.L. 1913, c. 49; C.S., s. 2490; 1925, c. 285, s. 1; 1931, c. 196; 1933, c. 101, s. 6; 1945, c. 182, s. 2; c. 196, s. 2; 1951, c. 926, s. 1; 1955, c. 386, s. 1; 1957, c. 564; 1961, c. 574; 1965, c. 700, s. 1; 1969, c. 1115, s. 1; 1975, c. 862, s. 7; 1983 (Reg. Sess., 1984), c. 1116, s. 43; 1989, c. 523, s. 7; 2000-169, s. 1; 2012-70, s. 12.)

§ 25-9-508. Effectiveness of financing statement if new debtor becomes bound by security agreement.

(a) Financing statement naming original debtor. - Except as otherwise provided in this section, a filed financing statement naming an original debtor is effective to perfect a security interest in collateral in which a new debtor has or acquires rights to the extent that the financing statement would have been effective had the original debtor acquired rights in the collateral.

(b) Financing statement becoming seriously misleading. - If the difference between the name of the original debtor and that of the new debtor causes a filed financing statement that is effective under subsection (a) of this section to be seriously misleading under G.S. 25-9-506:

(1)   The financing statement is effective to perfect a security interest in collateral acquired by the new debtor before, and within four months after, the new debtor becomes bound under G.S. 25-9-203(d); and

(2)   The financing statement is not effective to perfect a security interest in collateral acquired by the new debtor more than four months after the new debtor becomes bound under G.S. 25-9-203(d) unless an initial financing statement providing the name of the new debtor is filed before the expiration of that time.

(c)   When section not applicable. - This section does not apply to collateral as to which a filed financing statement remains effective against the new debtor under G.S. 25-9-507(a). (1967, c. 562, s. 3; 1975, c. 862, s. 7; 2000-169, s. 1.)

§ 25-9-509. Persons entitled to file a record.

(a)   Person entitled to file record. - A person may file an initial financing statement, amendment that adds collateral covered by a financing statement, or amendment that adds a debtor to a financing statement only if:

(1)   The debtor authorizes the filing in an authenticated record or pursuant to subsection (b) or (c) of this section; or

(2)   The person holds an agricultural lien that has become effective at the time of filing and the financing statement covers only collateral in which the person holds an agricultural lien.

(b)   Security agreement as authorization. - By authenticating or becoming bound as debtor by a security agreement, a debtor or new debtor authorizes the filing of an initial financing statement, and an amendment, covering:

(1)   The collateral described in the security agreement; and

(2)   Property that becomes collateral under G.S. 25-9-315(a)(2), whether or not the security agreement expressly covers proceeds.

(c) Acquisition of collateral as authorization. - By acquiring collateral in which a security interest or agricultural lien continues under G.S. 25-9-315(a)(1), a debtor authorizes the filing of an initial financing statement, and an amendment, covering the collateral and property that becomes collateral under G.S. 25-9-315(a)(2).

(d) Person entitled to file certain amendments. - A person may file an amendment other than an amendment that adds collateral covered by a financing statement or an amendment that adds a debtor to a financing statement only if:

(1) The secured party of record authorizes the filing; or

(2) The amendment is a termination statement for a financing statement as to which the secured party of record has failed to file or send a termination statement as required by G.S. 25-9-513(a) or (c), the debtor authorizes the filing, and the termination statement indicates that the debtor authorized it to be filed.

(e) Multiple secured parties of record. - If there is more than one secured party of record for a financing statement, each secured party of record may authorize the filing of an amendment under subsection (d) of this section. (1967, c. 562, s. 3; 1975, c. 862, s. 7; 2000-169, s. 1.)

§ 25-9-510. Effectiveness of filed record.

(a) Filed record effective if authorized. - A filed record is effective only to the extent that it was filed by a person that may file it under G.S. 25-9-509.

(b) Authorization by one secured party of record. - A record authorized by one secured party of record does not affect the financing statement with respect to another secured party of record.

(c) Continuation statement not timely filed. - A continuation statement that is not filed within the six-month period prescribed by G.S. 25-9-515(d) is ineffective. (2000-169, s. 1.)

§ 25-9-511. Secured party of record.

(a) Secured party of record. - A secured party of record with respect to a financing statement is a person whose name is provided as the name of the secured party or a representative of the secured party in an initial financing statement that has been filed. If an initial financing statement is filed under G.S. 25-9-514(a), the assignee named in the initial financing statement is the secured party of record with respect to the financing statement.

(b) Amendment naming secured party of record. - If an amendment of a financing statement which provides the name of a person as a secured party or a representative of a secured party is filed, the person named in the amendment is a secured party of record. If an amendment is filed under G.S. 25-9-514(b), the assignee named in the amendment is a secured party of record.

(c) Amendment deleting secured party of record. - A person remains a secured party of record until the filing of an amendment of the financing statement which deletes the person. (2000-169, s. 1.)

§ 25-9-512. Amendment of financing statement.

(a) Amendment of information in financing statement. - Subject to G.S. 25-9-509, a person may add or delete collateral covered by, continue or terminate the effectiveness of, or, subject to subsection (e) of this section, otherwise amend the information provided in, a financing statement by filing an amendment that:

(1) Identifies, by its file number, the initial financing statement to which the amendment relates; and

(2) If the amendment relates to an initial financing statement filed in a filing office described in G.S. 25-9-501(a)(1), provides the name of the debtor and the information specified in G.S. 25-9-502(b).

(b) Period of effectiveness not affected. - Except as otherwise provided in G.S. 25-9-515, the filing of an amendment does not extend the period of effectiveness of the financing statement.

(c) Effectiveness of amendment adding collateral. - A financing statement that is amended by an amendment that adds collateral is effective as to the added collateral only from the date of the filing of the amendment.

(d) Effectiveness of amendment adding debtor. - A financing statement that is amended by an amendment that adds a debtor is effective as to the added debtor only from the date of the filing of the amendment.

(e) Certain amendments ineffective. - An amendment is ineffective to the extent it:

(1) Purports to delete all debtors and fails to provide the name of a debtor to be covered by the financing statement; or

(2) Purports to delete all secured parties of record and fails to provide the name of a new secured party of record. (1899, cc. 17, 247; 1901, cc. 329, 704; 1903, c. 489; 1905, cc. 226, 319; Rev., s. 2055; 1907, c. 843; 1909, c. 532; P.L. 1913, c. 49; C.S., s. 2490; 1925, c. 285, s. 1; 1931, c. 196; 1933, c. 101, s. 6; 1945, c. 182, s. 2; c. 196, s. 2; 1951, c. 926, s. 1; 1955, c. 386, s. 1; 1957, c. 564; 1961, c. 574; 1965, c. 700, s. 1; 1969, c. 1115, s. 1; 1975, c. 862, s. 7; 1983 (Reg. Sess., 1984), c. 1116, s. 43; 1989, c. 523, s. 7; 2000-169, s. 1.)

§ 25-9-513. Termination statement.

(a) Consumer goods. - A secured party shall cause the secured party of record for a financing statement to file a termination statement for the financing statement if the financing statement covers consumer goods and:

(1) There is no obligation secured by the collateral covered by the financing statement and no commitment to make an advance, incur an obligation, or otherwise give value; or

(2) The debtor did not authorize the filing of the initial financing statement.

(b) Time for compliance with subsection (a). - To comply with subsection (a) of this section, a secured party shall cause the secured party of record to file the termination statement:

(1) Within one month after there is no obligation secured by the collateral covered by the financing statement and no commitment to make an advance, incur an obligation, or otherwise give value; or

(2) If earlier, within 20 days after the secured party receives an authenticated demand from a debtor.

(c) Other collateral. - In cases not governed by subsection (a) of this section, within 20 days after a secured party receives an authenticated demand from a debtor, the secured party shall cause the secured party of record for a financing statement to send to the debtor a termination statement for the financing statement or file the termination statement in the filing office if:

(1) Except in the case of a financing statement covering accounts or chattel paper that has been sold or goods that are the subject of a consignment, there is no obligation secured by the collateral covered by the financing statement and no commitment to make an advance, incur an obligation, or otherwise give value;

(2) The financing statement covers accounts or chattel paper that has been sold but as to which the account debtor or other person obligated has discharged its obligation;

(3) The financing statement covers goods that were the subject of a consignment to the debtor but are not in the debtor's possession; or

(4) The debtor did not authorize the filing of the initial financing statement.

(d) Effect of filing termination statement. - Except as otherwise provided in G.S. 25-9-510, upon the filing of a termination statement with the filing office, the financing statement to which the termination statement relates ceases to be effective. Except as otherwise provided in G.S. 25-9-510, for purposes of G.S. 25-9-519(g), 25-9-522(a), and 25-9-523(c), the filing with the filing office of a termination statement relating to a financing statement that indicates that the debtor is a transmitting utility also causes the effectiveness of the financing statement to lapse. (1945, c. 182, s. 5; c. 196, s. 3; 1961, c. 574; 1965, c. 700, s. 1; 1967, c. 562, s. 1; 1969, c. 1115, s. 1; 1973, c. 1316, ss. 2, 3; 1975, c. 862, s. 7; 1985, c. 221; 1989, c. 523, s. 5; 1991, c. 164, s. 2; 2000-169, s. 1.)

§ 25-9-514. Assignment of powers of secured party of record.

(a) Assignment reflected on initial financing statement. - Except as otherwise provided in subsection (c) of this section, an initial financing statement may reflect an assignment of all of the secured party's power to authorize an amendment to the financing statement by providing the name and mailing address of the assignee as the name and address of the secured party.

(b) Assignment of filed financing statement. - Except as otherwise provided in subsection (c) of this section, a secured party of record may assign of record all or part of its power to authorize an amendment to a financing statement by filing in the filing office an amendment of the financing statement which:

(1) Identifies, by its file number, the initial financing statement to which it relates;

(2) Provides the name of the assignor; and

(3) Provides the name and mailing address of the assignee.

(c) Assignment of record of mortgage. - An assignment of record of a security interest in a fixture covered by a record of a mortgage which is effective as a financing statement filed as a fixture filing under G.S. 25-9-502(c) may be made only by an assignment of record of the mortgage in the manner provided by law of this State other than this Chapter. (1965, c. 700, s. 1; 1967, c. 24, s. 23; 1969, c. 1115, s. 1; 1973, c. 1316, ss. 4, 5; 1975, c. 862, s. 7; 1983, c. 713, ss. 24, 25; 1987, c. 792, ss. 7, 8; 1989, c. 523, s. 6; 1997-456, s. 55.3; 1997-475, s. 5.5; 2000-169, s. 1.)

§ 25-9-515. Duration and effectiveness of financing statement; effect of lapsed financing statement.

(a) Five-year effectiveness. - Except as otherwise provided in subsections (b), (e), (f), and (g) of this section, a filed financing statement is effective for a period of five years after the date of filing.

(b) Public-finance or manufactured-home transaction. - Except as otherwise provided in subsections (e), (f), and (g) of this section, an initial financing statement filed in connection with a public-finance transaction or manufactured-home transaction is effective for a period of 30 years after the date of filing if it indicates that it is filed in connection with a public-finance transaction or manufactured-home transaction.

(c) Lapse and continuation of financing statement. - The effectiveness of a filed financing statement lapses on the expiration of the period of its effectiveness unless before the lapse a continuation statement is filed pursuant to subsection (d) of this section. Upon lapse, a financing statement ceases to be effective and any security interest or agricultural lien that was perfected by the financing statement becomes unperfected, unless the security interest is perfected otherwise. If the security interest or agricultural lien becomes unperfected upon lapse, it is deemed never to have been perfected as against a purchaser of the collateral for value.

(d) When continuation statement may be filed. - A continuation statement may be filed only within six months before the expiration of the five-year period specified in subsection (a) of this section or the 30-year period specified in subsection (b) of this section, whichever is applicable.

(e) Effect of filing continuation statement. - Except as otherwise provided in G.S. 25-9-510, upon timely filing of a continuation statement, the effectiveness of the initial financing statement continues for a period of five years commencing on the day on which the financing statement would have become ineffective in the absence of the filing. Upon the expiration of the five-year period, the financing statement lapses in the same manner as provided in subsection (c) of this section, unless, before the lapse, another continuation statement is filed pursuant to subsection (d) of this section. Succeeding continuation statements may be filed in the same manner to continue the effectiveness of the initial financing statement.

(f) Transmitting utility financing statement. - If a debtor is a transmitting utility and a filed initial financing statement so indicates, the financing statement is effective until a termination statement is filed.

(g) Record of mortgage as financing statement. - A record of a mortgage that is effective as a financing statement filed as a fixture filing under G.S. 25-9-502(c) remains effective as a financing statement filed as a fixture filing until the mortgage is released or satisfied of record or its effectiveness otherwise terminates as to the real property. (1866-7, c. 1, s. 1; 1872-3, c. 133, s. 1; Code, s. 1799; 1893, c. 9; Rev., s. 2052; C.S., s. 2480; 1925, c. 302, s. 1; 1927, c. 22; 1935, c. 205; 1945, c. 182, ss. 2, 4; c. 196, s. 2; 1955, c. 386, ss. 1, 2; c.

816; 1957, cc. 564, 999; 1961, c. 574; 1965, c. 700, s. 1; 1967, c. 562, s. 1; 1969, c. 1115, s. 1; 1971, c. 1170; 1973, c. 1316, s. 1; 1975, c. 862, s. 7; 1977, cc. 156, 295; 1983, c. 713, s. 23; 1987, c. 792, s. 6; 1989, c. 523, s. 4; 1991, c. 164, s. 1; 1997-456, s. 55.3; 1997-475, s. 5.4; 2000-169, s. 1; 2012-70, s. 13.)

§ 25-9-516. What constitutes filing; effectiveness of filing.

(a) What constitutes filing. - Except as otherwise provided in subsection (b) of this section, communication of a record to a filing office and tender of the filing fee or acceptance of the record by the filing office constitutes filing.

(b) Refusal to accept record; filing does not occur. - Filing does not occur with respect to a record that a filing office refuses to accept because:

(1) The record is not communicated by a method or medium of communication authorized by the filing office;

(2) An amount equal to or greater than the applicable filing fee is not tendered;

(3) The filing office is unable to index the record because:

a. In the case of an initial financing statement, the record does not provide a name for the debtor;

b. In the case of an amendment or information statement, the record:

1. Does not identify the initial financing statement as required by G.S. 25-9-512 or G.S. 25-9-518, as applicable; or

2. Identifies an initial financing statement whose effectiveness has lapsed under G.S. 25-9-515;

c. In the case of an initial financing statement that provides the name of a debtor identified as an individual or an amendment that provides a name of a debtor identified as an individual which was not previously provided in the financing statement to which the record relates, the record does not identify the debtor's surname; or

d. In the case of a record filed in the filing office described in G.S. 25-9-501(a)(1), the record does not provide a sufficient description of the real property to which it relates;

(4) In the case of an initial financing statement or an amendment that adds a secured party of record, the record does not provide a name and mailing address for the secured party of record;

(5) In the case of an initial financing statement or an amendment that provides a name of a debtor which was not previously provided in the financing statement to which the amendment relates, the record does not:

a. Provide a mailing address for the debtor; or

b. Indicate whether the name provided as the name of the debtor is the name of an individual or an organization;

c. Repealed by Session Laws 2012-70, s. 14, effective July 1, 2013.

(6) In the case of an assignment reflected in an initial financing statement under G.S. 25-9-514(a) or an amendment filed under G.S. 25-9-514(b), the record does not provide a name and mailing address for the assignee;

(7) In the case of a continuation statement, the record is not filed within the six-month period prescribed by G.S. 25-9-515(d); or

(8) In the case of a record presented for filing at the Department of the Secretary of State, the Secretary of State determines that the record is not created pursuant to this Chapter or is otherwise intended for an improper purpose, such as to hinder, harass, or otherwise wrongfully interfere with any person.

(c) Rules applicable to subsection (b). - For purposes of subsection (b) of this section:

(1) A record does not provide information if the filing office is unable to read or decipher the information; and

(2) A record that does not indicate that it is an amendment or identify an initial financing statement to which it relates, as required by G.S. 25-9-512, 25-9-514, or 25-9-518, is an initial financing statement.

(d) Refusal to accept record; record effective as filed record. - A record that is communicated to the filing office with tender of the filing fee, but which the filing office refuses to accept for a reason other than one set forth in subsection (b) of this section, is effective as a filed record except as against a purchaser of the collateral which gives value in reasonable reliance upon the absence of the record from the files. (1866-7, c. 1, s. 1; 1872-3, c. 133, s. 1; Code, s. 1799; 1893, c. 9; Rev., s. 2052; C.S., s. 2480; 1925, c. 302, s. 1; 1927, c. 22; 1935, c. 205; 1945, c. 182, ss. 2, 4; c. 196, s. 2; 1955, c. 386, ss. 1, 2; c. 816; 1957, cc. 564, 999; 1961, c. 574; 1965, c. 700, s. 1; 1967, c. 562, s. 1; 1969, c. 1115, s. 1; 1971, c. 1170; 1973, c. 1316, s. 1; 1975, c. 862, s. 7; 1977, cc. 156, 295; 1983, c. 713, s. 23; 1987, c. 792, s. 6; 1989, c. 523, s. 4; 1991, c. 164, s. 1; 1997-456, s. 55.3; 1997-475, s. 5.4; 2000-169, s. 1; 2001-231, s. 1; 2012-70, s. 14.)

§ 25-9-517. Effect of indexing errors.

The failure of the filing office to index a record correctly does not affect the effectiveness of the filed record. (2000-169, s. 1.)

§ 25-9-518. Claim concerning inaccurate or wrongfully filed record.

(a) Statement With Respect to Record Indexed Under Person's Name. - A person may file in the filing office an information statement with respect to a record indexed there under the person's name if the person believes that the record is inaccurate or was wrongfully filed.

(b) Contents of Statement Under Subsection (a). - An information statement under subsection (a) of this section must:

(1) Identify the record to which it relates by the file number assigned to the initial financing statement to which the record relates;

(2) Indicate that it is an information statement; and

(3) Provide the basis for the person's belief that the record is inaccurate and indicate the manner in which the person believes the record should be amended to cure any inaccuracy or provide the basis for the person's belief that the record

was wrongfully filed. An information statement that is subject to the provisions of subsection (b1) of this section shall include a written certification, under oath, by the person that the contents of the information statement are true and accurate to the best of the person's knowledge.

(b1)   In the case of an information statement alleging that a previously filed record was wrongfully filed and that it should have been rejected under G.S. 25-9-516(b)(8), the Secretary of State shall, without undue delay, determine whether the contested record was wrongfully filed and should have been rejected. In order to determine whether the record was wrongfully filed, the Secretary of State may require the person filing the information statement and the secured party to provide any additional relevant information requested by the Secretary of State, including an original or a copy of any security agreement that is related to the record. If the Secretary of State finds that the record was wrongfully filed and should have been rejected under G.S. 25-9-516(b)(8), the Secretary of State shall cancel the record and it shall be void and of no effect.

(b2)   Statement by Secured Party of Record. - A person may file in the filing office an information statement with respect to a record filed there if the person is a secured party of record with respect to the financing statement to which the record relates and believes that the person that filed the record was not entitled to do so under G.S. 25-9-509(d).

(b3)   Contents of Statement Under Subsection (b2). - An information statement under subsection (b2) of this section must:

(1)   Identify the record to which it relates by the file number assigned to the initial financing statement to which the record relates;

(2)   Indicate that it is an information statement; and

(3)   Provide the basis for the person's belief that the person that filed the record was not entitled to do so under G.S. 25-9-509(d).

(c)   Record not affected by information statement. - The filing of an information statement does not affect the effectiveness of an initial financing statement or other filed record. (2000-169, s. 1; 2001-231, ss. 2, 3; 2012-70, s. 15.)

SUBPART 2. Duties and Operation of Filing Office.

§ 25-9-519. Numbering, maintaining, and indexing records; communicating information provided in records.

(a)   Filing office duties. - For each record filed in a filing office, the filing office shall:

(1)   Assign a unique number to the filed record;

(2)   Create a record that bears the number assigned to the filed record and the date and time of filing;

(3)   Maintain the filed record for public inspection; and

(4)   Index the filed record in accordance with subsections (c), (d), and (e) of this section.

(b)   File number. - Except as otherwise provided in subsection (i) of this section, a file number assigned after January 1, 2003, must include a digit that:

(1)   Is mathematically derived from or related to the other digits of the file number; and

(2)   Aids the filing office in determining whether a number communicated as the file number includes a single-digit or transpositional error.

(c)   Indexing: general. - Except as otherwise provided in subsections (d) and (e) of this section, the filing office shall:

(1)   Index an initial financing statement according to the name of the debtor and index all filed records relating to the initial financing statement in a manner that associates with one another an initial financing statement and all filed records relating to the initial financing statement; and

(2)   Index a record that provides a name of a debtor which was not previously provided in the financing statement to which the record relates also according to the name that was not previously provided.

(d) Indexing: real-property-related financing statement. - If a financing statement is filed as a fixture filing or covers as-extracted collateral or timber to be cut, the filing office shall index it:

(1) Under the names of the debtor and of each owner of record shown on the financing statement as if they were the mortgagors under a mortgage of the real property described; and

(2) To the extent that the law of this State provides for indexing of records of mortgages under the name of the mortgagee, under the name of the secured party as if the secured party were the mortgagee thereunder, or, if indexing is by description, as if the financing statement were a record of a mortgage of the real property described.

(e) Indexing: real-property-related assignment. - If a financing statement is filed as a fixture filing or covers as-extracted collateral or timber to be cut, the filing office shall index an assignment filed under G.S. 25-9-514(a) or an amendment filed under G.S. 25-9-514(b):

(1) Under the name of the assignor as grantor; and

(2) To the extent that the law of this State provides for indexing a record of the assignment of a mortgage under the name of the assignee, under the name of the assignee.

(f) Retrieval and association capability. - The filing office shall maintain a capability:

(1) To retrieve a record by the name of the debtor and by the file number assigned to the initial financing statement to which the record relates; and

(2) To associate and retrieve with one another an initial financing statement and each filed record relating to the initial financing statement.

(g) Removal of debtor's name. - The filing office may not remove a debtor's name from the index until one year after the effectiveness of a financing statement naming the debtor lapses under G.S. 25-9-515 with respect to all secured parties of record.

(h) Timeliness of filing office performance. - The filing office shall perform the acts required by subsections (a) through (e) of this section at the time and in the manner prescribed by filing-office rule, but after January 1, 2003, not later than three business days after the filing office receives the record in question.

(i) Inapplicability to real-property-related filing office. - Subsection (b) of this section does not apply to a filing office described in G.S. 25-9-501(a)(1). (1866-7, c. 1, s. 1; 1872-3, c. 133, s. 1; Code, s. 1799; 1893, c. 9; Rev., s. 2052; C.S., s. 2480; 1925, c. 302, s. 1; 1927, c. 22; 1935, c. 205; 1945, c. 182, ss. 2, 4; c. 196, s. 2; 1955, c. 386, ss. 1, 2; c. 816; 1957, cc. 564, 999; 1961, c. 574; 1965, c. 700, s. 1; 1967, c. 562, s. 1; 1969, c. 1115, s. 1; 1971, c. 1170; 1973, c. 1316, s. 1; 1975, c. 862, s. 7; 1977, cc. 156, 295; 1983, c. 713, s. 23; 1987, c. 792, s. 6; 1989, c. 523, s. 4; 1991, c. 164, s. 1; 1997-456, s. 55.3; 1997-475, s. 5.4; 2000-169, s. 1.)

§ 25-9-520. Acceptance, refusal to accept record, and cancellation of record.

(a) Mandatory refusal to accept record. - A filing office shall refuse to accept a record for filing for a reason set forth in G.S. 25-9-516(b) and may refuse to accept a record for filing only for a reason set forth in G.S. 25-9-516(b).

(b) Communication concerning refusal. - If a filing office refuses to accept a record for filing or cancels a record under G.S. 25-9-518(b1), it shall communicate to the person that presented the record the fact of and reason for the refusal or cancellation and the date and time the record would have been filed had the filing office accepted it. The communication must be made at the time and in the manner prescribed by filing-office rule but in no event more than three business days after the filing office receives or cancels the record.

(c) When filed financing statement effective. - A filed financing statement satisfying G.S. 25-9-502(a) and (b) is effective, even if the filing office is required to refuse to accept it for filing under subsection (a) of this section. However, G.S. 25-9-338 applies to a filed financing statement providing information described in G.S. 25-9-516(b)(5) which is incorrect at the time the financing statement is filed.

(d) Separate application to multiple debtors. - If a record communicated to a filing office provides information that relates to more than one debtor, this Part applies as to each debtor separately.

(e) Appeal. -

(1)   If the Secretary of State refuses to accept a record for filing pursuant to G.S. 25-9-516(b)(8) or cancels a wrongfully filed record pursuant to G.S. 25-9-518(b1), the secured party may file an appeal within 30 days after the refusal or cancellation in the Superior Court of Wake County. Filing a petition requesting to be allowed to file the document commences the appeal. The petition shall be filed with the court and with the Secretary of State and shall have the record attached to it. Upon the commencement of an appeal, it shall be set for hearing at the earliest possible time and shall take precedence over all matters except older matters of the same character. The appeal to the Superior Court is not governed by Article 3, 3A, or 4 of Chapter 150B of the General Statutes and shall be determined upon such further notice and opportunity to be heard, if any, as the court may deem appropriate under the circumstances. The court shall permit the joinder of any interested party that would be allowed under the Rules of Civil Procedure.

(2)   Upon consideration of the petition and other appropriate pleadings, the court may order the Secretary of State to file the record or take other action the court considers appropriate, including the entry of orders affirming, reversing, or otherwise modifying the decision of the Secretary of State. The court may order any other relief, including equitable relief, as may be appropriate.

(3)   The court's final decision may be appealed as in other civil proceedings. (2000-169, s. 1; 2001-231, s. 4.)

§ 25-9-521. Uniform form of written financing statement and amendment.

(a)   Initial financing statement form. - A filing office that accepts written records may not refuse to accept a written initial financing statement in the following form and format except for a reason set forth in G.S. 25-9-516(b):

UCC FINANCING STATEMENT (Form UCC1) (Rev. 04-20-11)

(b) Amendment form. - A filing office that accepts written records may not refuse to accept a written record in the following form and format except for a reason set forth in G.S. 25-9-516(b):

UCC FINANCING STATEMENT AMENDMENT (Form UCC3) (Rev. 04-20-11).pdf

(1899, cc. 17, 247; 1901, cc. 329, 704; 1903, c. 489; 1905, cc. 226, 319; Rev., s. 2055; 1907, c. 843; 1909, c. 532; P.L. 1913, c. 49; C.S., s. 2490; 1925, c. 285, s. 1; 1931, c. 196; 1933, c. 101, s. 6; 1945, c. 182, s. 2; c. 196, s. 2; 1951, c. 926, s. 1; 1955, c. 386, s. 1; 1957, c. 564; 1961, c. 574; 1965, c. 700, s. 1; 1969, c. 1115, s. 1; 1975, c. 862, s. 7; 1983 (Reg. Sess., 1984), c. 1116, s. 43; 1989, c. 523, s. 7; 2000-169, ss. 1, 2(a)-(c); 2012-70, s. 16.)

§ 25-9-522. Maintenance and destruction of records.

(a) Post-lapse maintenance and retrieval of information. - The filing office shall maintain a record of the information provided in a filed financing statement for at least one year after the effectiveness of the financing statement has lapsed under G.S. 25-9-515 with respect to all secured parties of record. The record must be retrievable by using the name of the debtor and by using the file number assigned to the initial financing statement to which the record relates.

(b) Destruction of written records. - Except to the extent that a statute governing disposition of public records provides otherwise, the filing office immediately may destroy any written record evidencing a financing statement. However, if the filing office destroys a written record, it shall maintain another record of the financing statement which complies with subsection (a) of this section. (1866-7, c. 1, s. 1; 1872-3, c. 133, s. 1; Code, s. 1799; 1893, c. 9; Rev., s. 2052; C.S., s. 2480; 1925, c. 302, s. 1; 1927, c. 22; 1935, c. 205; 1945, c. 182, ss. 2, 4; c. 196, s. 2; 1955, c. 386, ss. 1, 2; c. 816; 1957, cc. 564, 999; 1961, c. 574; 1965, c. 700, s. 1; 1967, c. 562, s. 1; 1969, c. 1115, s. 1; 1971, c. 1170; 1973, c. 1316, s. 1; 1975, c. 862, s. 7; 1977, cc. 156, 295; 1983, c. 713, s. 23; 1987, c. 792, s. 6; 1989, c. 523, s. 4; 1991, c. 164, s. 1; 1997-456, s. 55.3; 1997-475, s. 5.4; 2000-169, s. 1.)

§ 25-9-523. Information from filing office.

(a) Acknowledgment of filing written record. - If a person that files a written record requests an acknowledgment of the filing, the filing office shall send to the person an image of the record showing the number assigned to the record pursuant to G.S. 25-9-519(a)(1) and the date and time of the filing of the record. However, if the person furnishes a copy of the record to the filing office, the filing office may instead:

(1) Note upon the copy the number assigned to the record pursuant to G.S. 25-9-519(a)(1) and the date and time of the filing of the record; and

(2) Send the copy to the person.

(b) Acknowledgment of filing other record. - If a person files a record other than a written record, the filing office shall communicate to the person an acknowledgment that provides:

(1) The information in the record;

(2) The number assigned to the record pursuant to G.S. 25-9-519(a)(1); and

(3) The date and time of the filing of the record.

(c) Communication of requested information. - Except as otherwise provided in subsection (g) of this section, the filing office shall communicate or otherwise make available in a record, for which it shall not be liable, the following information to any person that requests it:

(1) Whether there is on file on a date and time specified by the filing office, but not a date earlier than three business days before the filing office receives the request, any financing statement that:

a. Designates a particular debtor;

b. Has not lapsed under G.S. 25-9-515 with respect to all secured parties of record; and

c. If the request so states, has lapsed under G.S. 25-9-515 and a record of which is maintained by the filing office under G.S. 25-9-522(a);

(2) The date and time of filing of each financing statement; and

(3) The information provided in each financing statement.

(d) Medium for communicating information. - In complying with its duty under subsection (c) of this section, the filing office may communicate information in any medium. However, if requested, the filing office shall communicate information by issuing a record that can be admitted into evidence in the courts of this State without extrinsic evidence of its authenticity.

(e) Timeliness of filing office performance. - The filing office shall perform the acts required by subsections (a) through (d) of this section at the time and in the manner prescribed by filing-office rule, but after January 1, 2003, for a filing office described in G.S. 25-9-501(a)(2), not later than three business days after the filing office receives the request.

(f) Reserved.

(g) Inapplicability to real-property-related filing office. - Subsection (c) of this section does not apply to a filing office described in G.S. 25-9-501(a)(1) with respect to financing statements filed on or after the effective date of this act. (1965, c. 700, s. 1; 1967, c. 562, s. 1; 1973, c. 1316, s. 7; 1975, c. 862, s. 7; 1983, c. 713, ss. 27, 28; 1987, c. 792, s. 10; 1997-456, s. 55.3; 1997-475, s. 5.7; 2000-169, s. 1(d).)

§ 25-9-524. Delay by filing office.

Delay by the filing office beyond a time limit prescribed by this Part is excused if:

(1) The delay is caused by interruption of communication or computer facilities, war, emergency conditions, failure of equipment, or other circumstances beyond control of the filing office; and

(2) The filing office exercises reasonable diligence under the circumstances. (2000-169, s. 1.)

§ 25-9-525. Fees.

(a)   Initial financing statement or other record: general rule. - Except as otherwise provided in subsection (e) of this section, the fee for filing and indexing a record under this Part is:

(1)   Thirty-eight dollars ($38.00) if the record is communicated in writing and consists of one or two pages;

(2)   Forty-five dollars ($45.00) if the record is communicated in writing and consists of more than two pages, plus two dollars ($2.00) for each page over 10 pages; and

(3)   Thirty dollars ($30.00) if the record is communicated by another medium authorized by filing-office rule.

(b)   Reserved.

(c)   Number of names. - The number of names required to be indexed does not affect the amount of the fee in subsection (a) of this section.

(d)   Response to information request. - The fee for responding to a request for information from the filing office, including for communicating whether there is on file any financing statement naming a particular debtor, is:

(1)   Thirty-eight dollars ($38.00) if the request is communicated in writing; and

(2)   Thirty dollars ($30.00) if the request is communicated by another medium authorized by filing-office rule.

Upon request the filing office shall furnish a copy of any filed financing statement or statement of assignment for a uniform fee of two dollars ($2.00) per page. This subsection does not require that a fee be charged for remote access searching of the filing office database.

(e)   Record of mortgage. - This section does not require a fee with respect to a record of a mortgage which is effective as a financing statement filed as a fixture filing or as a financing statement covering as-extracted collateral or timber to be cut under G.S. 25-9-502(c). However, the recording and satisfaction fees that otherwise would be applicable to the record of the mortgage apply. (1866-7, c. 1, s. 1; 1872-3, c. 133, s. 1; Code, s. 1799; 1893, c. 9; Rev., s. 2052; C.S., s. 2480; 1925, c. 302, s. 1; 1927, c. 22; 1935, c. 205; 1945, c. 182, ss. 2, 4; c. 196, s. 2; 1955, c. 386, ss. 1, 2; c. 816; 1957, cc. 564, 999; 1961, c. 574; 1965, c. 700, s. 1; 1967, c. 562, s. 1; 1969, c. 1115, s. 1; 1971, c. 1170; 1973, c. 1316, s. 1; 1975, c. 862, s. 7; 1977, cc. 156, 295; 1983, c. 713, s. 23; 1987, c. 792, s. 6; 1989, c. 523, s. 4; 1991, c. 164, s. 1; 1997-456, s. 55.3; 1997-475, s. 5.4; 2000-169, s. 1; 2003-284, ss. 35B.1(a), 35B.1(b).)

§ 25-9-526. Filing-office rules.

(a) Adoption of filing-office rules. - The Secretary of State shall adopt and publish rules to implement the Secretary of State's responsibilities under this Part. The filing-office rules must be consistent with this Article.

(b) Harmonization of rules. - To keep the filing-office rules and practices of the filing office in harmony with the rules and practices of filing offices in other jurisdictions that enact substantially this Part, and to keep the technology used by the filing office compatible with the technology used by filing offices in other jurisdictions that enact substantially this Part, the Secretary of State, so far as is consistent with the purposes, policies, and provisions of this Article, in adopting, amending, and repealing filing-office rules, may:

(1) Consult with filing offices in other jurisdictions that enact substantially this Part;

(2) Consult the most recent version of the Model Rules promulgated by the International Association of Corporate Administrators or any successor organization; and

(3) Take into consideration the rules and practices of, and the technology used by, filing offices in other jurisdictions that enact substantially this Part. (2000-169, s. 1.)

§ 25-9-527. Reserved for future codification purposes.

PART 6.

DEFAULT.

SUBPART 1. Default and Enforcement of Security Interest.

§ 25-9-601. Rights after default; judicial enforcement; consignor or buyer of accounts, chattel paper, payment intangibles, or promissory notes.

(a) Rights of secured party after default. - After default, a secured party has the rights provided in this Part and, except as otherwise provided in G.S. 25-9-602, those provided by agreement of the parties. A secured party:

(1) May reduce a claim to judgment, foreclose, or otherwise enforce the claim, security interest, or agricultural lien by any available judicial procedure; and

(2) If the collateral is documents, may proceed either as to the documents or as to the goods they cover.

(b) Rights and duties of secured party in possession or control. - A secured party in possession of collateral or control of collateral under G.S. 25-7-106, 25-9-104, 25-9-105, 25-9-106, or 25-9-107 has the rights and duties provided in G.S. 25-9-207.

(c) Rights cumulative; simultaneous exercise. - The rights under subsections (a) and (b) of this section are cumulative and may be exercised simultaneously.

(d) Rights of debtor and obligor. - Except as otherwise provided in subsection (g) of this section and G.S. 25-9-605, after default, a debtor and an obligor have the rights provided in this Part and by agreement of the parties.

(e) Lien of levy after judgment. - If a secured party has reduced its claim to judgment, the lien of any levy that may be made upon the collateral by virtue of an execution based upon the judgment relates back to the earliest of:

(1) The date of perfection of the security interest or agricultural lien in the collateral;

(2)   The date of filing a financing statement covering the collateral; or

(3)   Any date specified in a statute under which the agricultural lien was created.

(f)   Execution sale. - A sale pursuant to an execution is a foreclosure of the security interest or agricultural lien by judicial procedure within the meaning of this section. A secured party may purchase at the sale and thereafter hold the collateral free of any other requirements of this Article.

(g)   Consignor or buyer of certain rights to payment. - Except as otherwise provided in G.S. 25-9-607(c), this Part imposes no duties upon a secured party that is a consignor or is a buyer of accounts, chattel paper, payment intangibles, or promissory notes. (1866-7, c. 1, s. 2; 1872-3, c. 133, s. 2; 1883, c. 88; Code, s. 1800; 1893, c. 9; Rev., s. 2054; C.S., s. 2488; 1961, c. 574; 1965, c. 700, s. 1; 1975, c. 862, s. 7; 2000-169, s. 1; 2006-112, s. 55.)

§ 25-9-602. Waiver and variance of rights and duties.

Except as otherwise provided in G.S. 25-9-624, to the extent that they give rights to a debtor or obligor and impose duties on a secured party, the debtor or obligor may not waive or vary the rules stated in the following listed sections:

(1)   G.S. 25-9-207(b)(4)c., which deals with use and operation of the collateral by the secured party;

(2)   G.S. 25-9-210, which deals with requests for an accounting and requests concerning a list of collateral and statement of account;

(3)   G.S. 25-9-607(c), which deals with collection and enforcement of collateral;

(4)   G.S. 25-9-608(a) and G.S. 25-9-615(c) to the extent that they deal with application or payment of noncash proceeds of collection, enforcement, or disposition;

(5)   G.S. 25-9-608(a) and G.S. 25-9-615(d) to the extent that they require accounting for or payment of surplus proceeds of collateral;

(6) G.S. 25-9-609 to the extent that it imposes upon a secured party that takes possession of collateral without judicial process the duty to do so without breach of the peace;

(7) G.S. 25-9-610(b), 25-9-611, 25-9-613, and 25-9-614, which deal with disposition of collateral;

(8) G.S. 25-9-615(f), which deals with calculation of a deficiency or surplus when a disposition is made to the secured party, a person related to the secured party, or a secondary obligor;

(9) G.S. 25-9-616, which deals with explanation of the calculation of a surplus or deficiency;

(10) G.S. 25-9-620, 25-9-621, and 25-9-622, which deal with acceptance of collateral in satisfaction of obligation;

(11) G.S. 25-9-623, which deals with redemption of collateral;

(12) G.S. 25-9-624, which deals with permissible waivers; and

(13) G.S. 25-9-625 and G.S. 25-9-626, which deal with the secured party's liability for failure to comply with this Article. (1866-7, c. 1, s. 2; 1872-3, c. 133, s. 2; 1883, c. 88; Code, s. 1800; 1893, c. 9; Rev., s. 2054; C.S., s. 2488; 1961, c. 574; 1965, c. 700, s. 1; 1975, c. 862, s. 7; 2000-169, s. 1.)

§ 25-9-603. Agreement on standards concerning rights and duties.

(a) Agreed standards. - The parties may determine by agreement the standards measuring the fulfillment of the rights of a debtor or obligor and the duties of a secured party under a rule stated in G.S. 25-9-602 if the standards are not manifestly unreasonable.

(b) Agreed standards inapplicable to breach of peace. - Subsection (a) of this section does not apply to the duty under G.S. 25-9-609 to refrain from breaching the peace. (1866-7, c. 1, s. 2; 1872-3, c. 133, s. 2; 1883, c. 88; Code, s. 1800; 1893, c. 9; Rev., s. 2054; C.S., s. 2488; 1961, c. 574; 1965, c. 700, s. 1; 1975, c. 862, s. 7; 2000-169, s. 1.)

§ 25-9-604. Procedure if security agreement covers real property or fixtures.

(a) Enforcement: personal and real property. - If a security agreement covers both personal and real property, a secured party may proceed:

(1) Under this Part as to the personal property without prejudicing any rights with respect to the real property; or

(2) As to both the personal property and the real property in accordance with the rights with respect to the real property, in which case the other provisions of this Part do not apply.

(b) Enforcement: fixtures. - Subject to subsection (c) of this section, if a security agreement covers goods that are or become fixtures, a secured party may proceed:

(1) Under this Part; or

(2) In accordance with the rights with respect to real property, in which case the other provisions of this Part do not apply.

(c) Removal of fixtures. - Subject to the other provisions of this Part, if a secured party holding a security interest in fixtures has priority over all owners and encumbrancers of the real property, the secured party, after default, may remove the collateral from the real property.

(d) Injury caused by removal. - A secured party that removes collateral shall promptly reimburse any encumbrancer or owner of the real property, other than the debtor, for the cost of repair of any physical injury caused by the removal. The secured party need not reimburse the encumbrancer or owner for any diminution in value of the real property caused by the absence of the goods removed or by any necessity of replacing them. A person entitled to reimbursement may refuse permission to remove until the secured party gives adequate assurance for the performance of the obligation to reimburse. (1965, c. 700, s. 1; 1967, c. 562, s. 1; 1975, c. 862, s. 7; 2000-169, s. 1.)

§ 25-9-605. Unknown debtor or secondary obligor.

A secured party does not owe a duty based on its status as secured party:

(1) To a person that is a debtor or obligor, unless the secured party knows:

a. That the person is a debtor or obligor;

b. The identity of the person; and

c. How to communicate with the person; or

(2) To a secured party or lienholder that has filed a financing statement against a person, unless the secured party knows:

a. That the person is a debtor; and

b. The identity of the person. (2000-169, s. 1.)

§ 25-9-606. Time of default for agricultural lien.

For purposes of this Part, a default occurs in connection with an agricultural lien at the time the secured party becomes entitled to enforce the lien in accordance with the statute under which it was created. (2000-169, s. 1.)

§ 25-9-607. Collection and enforcement by secured party.

(a) Collection and enforcement generally. - If so agreed, and in any event after default, a secured party:

(1) May notify an account debtor or other person obligated on collateral to make payment or otherwise render performance to or for the benefit of the secured party;

(2) May take any proceeds to which the secured party is entitled under G.S. 25-9-315;

(3) May enforce the obligations of an account debtor or other person obligated on collateral and exercise the rights of the debtor with respect to the obligation of the account debtor or other person obligated on collateral to make payment or otherwise render performance to the debtor, and with respect to any property that secures the obligations of the account debtor or other person obligated on the collateral;

(4) If it holds a security interest in a deposit account perfected by control under G.S. 25-9-104(a)(1), may apply the balance of the deposit account to the obligation secured by the deposit account; and

(5) If it holds a security interest in a deposit account perfected by control under G.S. 25-9-104(a)(2) or (a)(3), may instruct the bank to pay the balance of the deposit account to or for the benefit of the secured party.

(b) Nonjudicial enforcement of mortgage. - If necessary to enable a secured party to exercise under subdivision (a)(3) of this section the right of a debtor to enforce a mortgage nonjudicially, the secured party may record in the office in which a record of the mortgage is recorded:

(1) A copy of the security agreement that creates or provides for a security interest in the obligation secured by the mortgage; and

(2) The secured party's sworn affidavit in recordable form stating that:

a. A default has occurred with respect to the obligation secured by the mortgage; and

b. The secured party is entitled to enforce the mortgage nonjudicially.

(c) Commercially reasonable collection and enforcement. - A secured party shall proceed in a commercially reasonable manner if the secured party:

(1) Undertakes to collect from or enforce an obligation of an account debtor or other person obligated on collateral; and

(2) Is entitled to charge back uncollected collateral or otherwise to full or limited recourse against the debtor or a secondary obligor.

(d) Expenses of collection and enforcement. - A secured party may deduct from the collections made pursuant to subsection (c) of this section reasonable expenses of collection and enforcement, including reasonable attorney's fees and legal expenses incurred by the secured party.

(e) Duties to secured party not affected. - This section does not determine whether an account debtor, bank, or other person obligated on collateral owes a duty to a secured party. (1961, c. 574; 1965, c. 700, s. 1; 1975, c. 862, s. 7; 2000-169, s. 1; 2012-70, s. 17.)

§ 25-9-608. Application of proceeds of collection or enforcement; liability for deficiency and right to surplus.

(a) Application of proceeds, surplus, and deficiency if obligation secured. - If a security interest or agricultural lien secures payment or performance of an obligation, the following rules apply:

(1) A secured party shall apply or pay over for application the cash proceeds of collection or enforcement under G.S. 25-9-607 in the following order to:

a. The reasonable expenses of collection and enforcement and, to the extent provided for by agreement and not prohibited by law, reasonable attorney's fees and legal expenses incurred by the secured party;

b. The satisfaction of obligations secured by the security interest or agricultural lien under which the collection or enforcement is made; and

c. The satisfaction of obligations secured by any subordinate security interest in or other lien on the collateral subject to the security interest or agricultural lien under which the collection or enforcement is made if the secured party receives an authenticated demand for proceeds before distribution of the proceeds is completed.

(2) If requested by a secured party, a holder of a subordinate security interest or other lien shall furnish reasonable proof of the interest or lien within a reasonable time. Unless the holder complies, the secured party need not comply with the holder's demand under sub-subdivision (a)(1)c. of this section.

(3) A secured party need not apply or pay over for application noncash proceeds of collection and enforcement under G.S. 25-9-607 unless the failure

to do so would be commercially unreasonable. A secured party that applies or pays over for application noncash proceeds shall do so in a commercially reasonable manner.

(4)   A secured party shall account to and pay a debtor for any surplus, and the obligor is liable for any deficiency.

(b)   No surplus or deficiency in sales of certain rights to payment. - If the underlying transaction is a sale of accounts, chattel paper, payment intangibles, or promissory notes, the debtor is not entitled to any surplus, and the obligor is not liable for any deficiency. (1961, c. 574; 1965, c. 700, s. 1; 1975, c. 862, s. 7; 2000-169, s. 1.)

§ 25-9-609. Secured party's right to take possession after default.

(a)   Possession; rendering equipment unusable; disposition on debtor's premises. - After default, a secured party:

(1)   May take possession of the collateral; and

(2)   Without removal, may render equipment unusable and dispose of collateral on a debtor's premises under G.S. 25-9-610.

(b)   Judicial and nonjudicial process. - A secured party may proceed under subsection (a) of this section:

(1)   Pursuant to judicial process; or

(2)   Without judicial process, if it proceeds without breach of the peace.

(c)   Assembly of collateral. - If so agreed, and in any event after default, a secured party may require the debtor to assemble the collateral and make it available to the secured party at a place to be designated by the secured party which is reasonably convenient to both parties. (1961, c. 574; 1965, c. 700, s. 1; 1975, c. 862, s. 7; 2000-169, s. 1.)

§ 25-9-610. Disposition of collateral after default.

(a) Disposition after default. - After default, a secured party may sell, lease, license, or otherwise dispose of any or all of the collateral in its present condition or following any commercially reasonable preparation or processing.

(b) Commercially reasonable disposition. - Every aspect of a disposition of collateral, including the method, manner, time, place, and other terms, must be commercially reasonable. If commercially reasonable, a secured party may dispose of collateral by public or private proceedings, by one or more contracts, as a unit or in parcels, and at any time and place and on any terms.

(c) Purchase by secured party. - A secured party may purchase collateral:

(1) At a public disposition; or

(2) At a private disposition only if the collateral is of a kind that is customarily sold on a recognized market or the subject of widely distributed standard price quotations.

(d) Warranties on disposition. - A contract for sale, lease, license, or other disposition includes the warranties relating to title, possession, quiet enjoyment, and the like which by operation of law accompany a voluntary disposition of property of the kind subject to the contract.

(e) Disclaimer of warranties. - A secured party may disclaim or modify warranties under subsection (d) of this section:

(1) In a manner that would be effective to disclaim or modify the warranties in a voluntary disposition of property of the kind subject to the contract of disposition; or

(2) By communicating to the purchaser a record evidencing the contract for disposition and including an express disclaimer or modification of the warranties.

(f) Record sufficient to disclaim warranties. - A record is sufficient to disclaim warranties under subsection (e) of this section if it indicates "There is no warranty relating to title, possession, quiet enjoyment, or the like in this disposition" or uses words of similar import. (1965, c. 700, s. 1; 1975, c. 862, s. 7; 2000-169, s. 1.)

§ 25-9-611. Notification before disposition of collateral.

(a)   "Notification date." - In this section, "notification date" means the earlier of the date on which:

(1)   A secured party sends to the debtor and any secondary obligor an authenticated notification of disposition; or

(2)   The debtor and any secondary obligor waive the right to notification.

(b)   Notification of disposition required. - Except as otherwise provided in subsection (d) of this section, a secured party that disposes of collateral under G.S. 25-9-610 shall send to the persons specified in subsection (c) of this section a reasonable authenticated notification of disposition.

(c)   Persons to be notified. - To comply with subsection (b) of this section, the secured party shall send an authenticated notification of disposition to:

(1)   The debtor;

(2)   Any secondary obligor; and

(3)   If the collateral is other than consumer goods:

a.   Any other person from which the secured party has received, before the notification date, an authenticated notification of a claim of an interest in the collateral;

b.   Any other secured party or lienholder that, 10 days before the notification date, held a security interest in or other lien on the collateral perfected by the filing of a financing statement that:

1.   Identified the collateral;

2.   Was indexed under the debtor's name as of that date; and

3.   Was filed in the office in which to file a financing statement against the debtor covering the collateral as of that date; and

c. Any other secured party that, 10 days before the notification date, held a security interest in the collateral perfected by compliance with a statute, regulation, or treaty described in G.S. 25-9-311(a).

(d) Subsection (b) inapplicable: perishable collateral; recognized market. - Subsection (b) of this section does not apply if the collateral is perishable or threatens to decline speedily in value or is of a type customarily sold on a recognized market.

(e) Compliance with sub-subdivision (c)(3)b. - A secured party complies with the requirement for notification prescribed by sub-subdivision (c)(3)b. of this section if:

(1) Not later than 20 days or earlier than 30 days before the notification date, the secured party requests, in a commercially reasonable manner, information concerning financing statements indexed under the debtor's name in the office indicated in sub-subdivision (c)(3)b. of this section; and

(2) Before the notification date, the secured party:

a. Did not receive a response to the request for information; or

b. Received a response to the request for information and sent an authenticated notification of disposition to each secured party or other lienholder named in that response whose financing statement covered the collateral. (1965, c. 700, s. 1; 1975, c. 862, s. 7; 2000-169, s. 1.)

§ 25-9-612. Timeliness of notification before disposition of collateral.

(a) Reasonable time is question of fact. - Except as otherwise provided in subsection (b) of this section, whether a notification is sent within a reasonable time is a question of fact.

(b) Ten-day period sufficient in nonconsumer transaction. - In a transaction other than a consumer transaction, a notification of disposition sent after default and 10 days or more before the earliest time of disposition set forth in the notification is sent within a reasonable time before the disposition. (2000-169, s. 1.)

§ 25-9-613. Contents and form of notification before disposition of collateral: general.

Except in a consumer-goods transaction, the following rules apply:

(1) The contents of a notification of disposition are sufficient if the notification:

a. Describes the debtor and the secured party;

b. Describes the collateral that is the subject of the intended disposition;

c. States the method of intended disposition;

d. States that the debtor is entitled to an accounting of the unpaid indebtedness and states the charge, if any, for an accounting; and

e. States the time and place of a public disposition or the time after which any other disposition is to be made.

(2) Whether the contents of a notification that lacks any of the information specified in subdivision (1) of this section are nevertheless sufficient is a question of fact.

(3) The contents of a notification providing substantially the information specified in subdivision (1) of this section are sufficient, even if the notification includes:

a. Information not specified by that subdivision; or

b. Minor errors that are not seriously misleading.

(4) A particular phrasing of the notification is not required.

(5) The following form of notification and the form appearing in G.S. 25-9-614(3), when completed, each provides sufficient information:

NOTIFICATION OF DISPOSITION OF COLLATERAL

To: [Name of debtor, obligor, or other person to which the notification is sent]

From: [Name, address, and telephone number of secured party]

Name of Debtor(s): [Include only if debtor(s) is/are not an addressee]

[For a public disposition:]

We will sell [or lease or license, as applicable] the [describe collateral] [to the highest qualified bidder] in public as follows:

Day and Date:_____

Time:_____

Place:_____

[For a private disposition:]

We will sell [or lease or license, as applicable] the [describe collateral] privately sometime after [day and date].

You are entitled to an accounting of the unpaid indebtedness secured by the property that we intend to sell [or lease or license, as applicable] [for a charge of $ _____]. You may request an accounting by calling us at [telephone number] (2000-169, s. 1.)

§ 25-9-614. Contents and form of notification before disposition of collateral: consumer-goods transaction.

In a consumer-goods transaction, the following rules apply:

(1)   A notification of disposition must provide the following information:

a. The information specified in G.S. 25-9-613(1);

b. A description of any liability for a deficiency of the person to which the notification is sent;

c. A telephone number from which the amount that must be paid to the secured party to redeem the collateral under G.S. 25-9-623 is available; and

d. A telephone number or mailing address from which additional information concerning the disposition and the obligation secured is available.

(2) A particular phrasing of the notification is not required.

(3) The following form of notification, when completed, provides sufficient information:

[Name and address of secured party]

[Date]

NOTICE OF OUR PLAN TO SELL PROPERTY

[Name and address of any obligor who is also a debtor]

Subject: [Identification of Transaction]

We have your [describe collateral], because you broke promises in our agreement.

[For a public disposition:]

We will sell [describe collateral] at public sale. A sale could include a lease or license. The sale will be held as follows:

Date:_____

Time:_____

Place:_____

You may attend the sale and bring bidders if you want.

[For a private disposition:]

We will sell [describe collateral] at private sale sometime after [date]. A sale could include a lease or license.

The money that we get from the sale (after paying our costs) will reduce the amount you owe. If we get less money than you owe, you [will or will not, as applicable] still owe us the difference. If we get more money than you owe, you will get the extra money, unless we must pay it to someone else.

You can get the property back at any time before we sell it by paying us the full amount you owe (not just the past due payments), including our expenses. To learn the exact amount you must pay, call us at [telephone number].

If you want us to explain to you in writing how we have figured the amount that you owe us, you may call us at [telephone number] or write us at [secured party's address] and request a written explanation. [We will charge you $_____ for the explanation if we sent you another written explanation of the amount you owe us within the last six months.]

If you need more information about the sale call us at [telephone number] [or write us at [secured party's address].

We are sending this notice to the following other people who have an interest in [describe collateral] or who owe money under your agreement:

[Names of all other debtors and obligors, if any]

(4)   A notification in the form of subdivision (3) of this section is sufficient, even if additional information appears at the end of the form.

(5)   A notification in the form of subdivision (3) of this section is sufficient, even if it includes errors in information not required by subdivision (1) of this section, unless the error is misleading with respect to rights arising under this Article.

(6)   If a notification under this section is not in the form of subdivision (3) of this section, law other than this Article determines the effect of including information not required by subdivision (1) of this section. (2000-169, s. 1.)

§ 25-9-615.   Application of proceeds of disposition; liability for deficiency and right to surplus.

(a)   Application of proceeds. - A secured party shall apply or pay over for application the cash proceeds of disposition under G.S. 25-9-610 in the following order to:

(1)   The reasonable expenses of retaking, holding, preparing for disposition, processing, and disposing, and, to the extent provided for by agreement and not prohibited by law, reasonable attorney's fees and legal expenses incurred by the secured party;

(2)   The satisfaction of obligations secured by the security interest or agricultural lien under which the disposition is made;

(3)   The satisfaction of obligations secured by any subordinate security interest in or other subordinate lien on the collateral if:

a. The secured party receives from the holder of the subordinate security interest or other lien an authenticated demand for proceeds before distribution of the proceeds is completed; and

b. In a case in which a consignor has an interest in the collateral, the subordinate security interest or other lien is senior to the interest of the consignor; and

(4) A secured party that is a consignor of the collateral if the secured party receives from the consignor an authenticated demand for proceeds before distribution of the proceeds is completed.

(b) Proof of subordinate interest. - If requested by a secured party, a holder of a subordinate security interest or other lien shall furnish reasonable proof of the interest or lien within a reasonable time. Unless the holder does so, the secured party need not comply with the holder's demand under subdivision (a)(3) of this section.

(c) Application of noncash proceeds. - A secured party need not apply or pay over for application noncash proceeds of disposition under G.S. 25-9-610 unless the failure to do so would be commercially unreasonable. A secured party that applies or pays over for application noncash proceeds shall do so in a commercially reasonable manner.

(d) Surplus or deficiency if obligation secured. - If the security interest under which a disposition is made secures payment or performance of an obligation, after making the payments and applications required by subsection (a) of this section and permitted by subsection (c) of this section:

(1) Unless subdivision (a)(4) of this section requires the secured party to apply or pay over cash proceeds to a consignor, the secured party shall account to and pay a debtor for any surplus; and

(2) The obligor is liable for any deficiency.

(e) No surplus or deficiency in sales of certain rights to payment. - If the underlying transaction is a sale of accounts, chattel paper, payment intangibles, or promissory notes:

(1) The debtor is not entitled to any surplus; and

(2) The obligor is not liable for any deficiency.

(f) Calculation of surplus or deficiency in disposition to person related to secured party. - The surplus or deficiency following a disposition is calculated based on the amount of proceeds that would have been realized in a disposition complying with this Part to a transferee other than the secured party, a person related to the secured party, or a secondary obligor if:

(1) The transferee in the disposition is the secured party, a person related to the secured party, or a secondary obligor; and

(2) The amount of proceeds of the disposition is significantly below the range of proceeds that a complying disposition to a person other than the secured party, a person related to the secured party, or a secondary obligor would have brought.

(g) Cash proceeds received by junior secured party. - A secured party that receives cash proceeds of a disposition in good faith and without knowledge that the receipt violates the rights of the holder of a security interest or other lien that is not subordinate to the security interest or agricultural lien under which the disposition is made:

(1) Takes the cash proceeds free of the security interest or other lien;

(2) Is not obligated to apply the proceeds of the disposition to the satisfaction of obligations secured by the security interest or other lien; and

(3) Is not obligated to account to or pay the holder of the security interest or other lien for any surplus. (1965, c. 700, s. 1; 1975, c. 862, s. 7; 2000-169, s. 1.)

§ 25-9-616. Explanation of calculation of surplus or deficiency.

(a) Definitions. - In this section:

(1) "Explanation" means a writing that:

a. States the amount of the surplus or deficiency;

b. Provides an explanation in accordance with subsection (c) of this section of how the secured party calculated the surplus or deficiency;

c. States, if applicable, that future debits, credits, charges, including additional credit service charges or interest, rebates, and expenses may affect the amount of the surplus or deficiency; and

d. Provides a telephone number or mailing address from which additional information concerning the transaction is available.

(2) "Request" means a record:

a. Authenticated by a debtor or consumer obligor;

b. Requesting that the recipient provide an explanation; and

c. Sent after disposition of the collateral under G.S. 25-9-610.

(b) Explanation of calculation. - In a consumer-goods transaction in which the debtor is entitled to a surplus or a consumer obligor is liable for a deficiency under G.S. 25-9-615, the secured party shall:

(1) Send an explanation to the debtor or consumer obligor, as applicable, after the disposition and:

a. Before or when the secured party accounts to the debtor and pays any surplus or first makes written demand on the consumer obligor after the disposition for payment of the deficiency; and

b. Within 14 days after receipt of a request; or

(2) In the case of a consumer obligor who is liable for a deficiency, within 14 days after receipt of a request, send to the consumer obligor a record waiving the secured party's right to a deficiency.

(c) Required information. - To comply with sub-subdivision (a)(1)b. of this section, a writing must provide the following information in the following order:

(1) The aggregate amount of obligations secured by the security interest under which the disposition was made, and, if the amount reflects a rebate of

unearned interest or credit service charge, an indication of that fact, calculated as of a specified date:

a. If the secured party takes or receives possession of the collateral after default, not more than 35 days before the secured party takes or receives possession; or

b. If the secured party takes or receives possession of the collateral before default or does not take possession of the collateral, not more than 35 days before the disposition;

(2) The amount of proceeds of the disposition;

(3) The aggregate amount of the obligations after deducting the amount of proceeds;

(4) The amount, in the aggregate or by type, and types of expenses, including expenses of retaking, holding, preparing for disposition, processing, and disposing of the collateral, and attorney's fees secured by the collateral which are known to the secured party and relate to the current disposition;

(5) The amount, in the aggregate or by type, and types of credits, including rebates of interest or credit service charges, to which the obligor is known to be entitled and which are not reflected in the amount in subdivision (1) of this subsection; and

(6) The amount of the surplus or deficiency.

(d) Substantial compliance. - A particular phrasing of the explanation is not required. An explanation complying substantially with the requirements of subsection (a) of this section is sufficient, even if it includes minor errors that are not seriously misleading.

(e) Charges for responses. - A debtor or consumer obligor is entitled without charge to one response to a request under this section during any six-month period in which the secured party did not send to the debtor or consumer obligor an explanation pursuant to subdivision (b)(1) of this section. The secured party may require payment of a charge not exceeding twenty-five dollars ($25.00) for each additional response. (2000-169, s. 1.)

§ 25-9-617. Rights of transferee of collateral.

(a) Effects of disposition. - A secured party's disposition of collateral after default:

(1) Transfers to a transferee for value all of the debtor's rights in the collateral;

(2) Discharges the security interest under which the disposition is made; and

(3) Discharges any subordinate security interest or other subordinate lien.

(b) Rights of good-faith transferee. - A transferee that acts in good faith takes free of the rights and interests described in subsection (a) of this section, even if the secured party fails to comply with this Article or the requirements of any judicial proceeding.

(c) Rights of other transferee. - If a transferee does not take free of the rights and interests described in subsection (a) of this section, the transferee takes the collateral subject to:

(1) The debtor's rights in the collateral;

(2) The security interest or agricultural lien under which the disposition is made; and

(3) Any other security interest or other lien. (1965, c. 700, s. 1; 1975, c. 862, s. 7; 2000-169, s. 1.)

§ 25-9-618. Rights and duties of certain secondary obligors.

(a) Rights and duties of secondary obligor. - A secondary obligor acquires the rights and becomes obligated to perform the duties of the secured party after the secondary obligor:

(1) Receives an assignment of a secured obligation from the secured party;

(2) Receives a transfer of collateral from the secured party and agrees to accept the rights and assume the duties of the secured party; or

(3) Is subrogated to the rights of a secured party with respect to collateral.

(b) Effect of assignment, transfer, or subrogation. - An assignment, transfer, or subrogation described in subsection (a) of this section:

(1) Is not a disposition of collateral under G.S. 25-9-610; and

(2) Relieves the secured party of further duties under this Article. (1965, c. 700, s. 1; 1975, c. 862, s. 7; 2000-169, s. 1.)

§ 25-9-619. Transfer of record or legal title.

(a) "Transfer statement." - In this section, "transfer statement" means a record authenticated by a secured party stating:

(1) That the debtor has defaulted in connection with an obligation secured by specified collateral;

(2) That the secured party has exercised its postdefault remedies with respect to the collateral;

(3) That, by reason of the exercise, a transferee has acquired the rights of the debtor in the collateral; and

(4) The name and mailing address of the secured party, debtor, and transferee.

(b) Effect of transfer statement. - A transfer statement entitles the transferee to the transfer of record of all rights of the debtor in the collateral specified in the statement in any official filing, recording, registration, or certificate-of-title system covering the collateral. If a transfer statement is presented with the applicable fee and request form to the official or office responsible for maintaining the system, the official or office shall:

(1) Accept the transfer statement;

(2)　Promptly amend its records to reflect the transfer; and

(3)　If applicable, issue a new appropriate certificate of title in the name of the transferee.

(c)　Transfer not a disposition; no relief of secured party's duties. - A transfer of the record or legal title to collateral to a secured party under subsection (b) of this section or otherwise is not of itself a disposition of collateral under this Article and does not of itself relieve the secured party of its duties under this Article. (2000-169, s. 1.)

§ 25-9-620. Acceptance of collateral in full or partial satisfaction of obligation; compulsory disposition of collateral.

(a)　Conditions to acceptance in satisfaction. - Except as otherwise provided in subsection (g) of this section, a secured party may accept collateral in full or partial satisfaction of the obligation it secures only if:

(1)　The debtor consents to the acceptance under subsection (c) of this section;

(2)　The secured party does not receive, within the time set forth in subsection (d) of this section, a notification of objection to the proposal authenticated by:

a.　A person to which the secured party was required to send a proposal under G.S. 25-9-621; or

b.　Any other person, other than the debtor, holding an interest in the collateral subordinate to the security interest that is the subject of the proposal;

(3)　If the collateral is consumer goods, the collateral is not in the possession of the debtor when the debtor consents to the acceptance; and

(4)　Subsection (e) of this section does not require the secured party to dispose of the collateral or the debtor waives the requirement pursuant to G.S. 25-9-624.

(b) Purported acceptance ineffective. - A purported or apparent acceptance of collateral under this section is ineffective unless:

(1) The secured party consents to the acceptance in an authenticated record or sends a proposal to the debtor; and

(2) The conditions of subsection (a) of this section are met.

(c) Debtor's consent. - For purposes of this section:

(1) A debtor consents to an acceptance of collateral in partial satisfaction of the obligation it secures only if the debtor agrees to the terms of the acceptance in a record authenticated after default; and

(2) A debtor consents to an acceptance of collateral in full satisfaction of the obligation it secures only if the debtor agrees to the terms of the acceptance in a record authenticated after default or the secured party:

a. Sends to the debtor after default a proposal that is unconditional or subject only to a condition that collateral not in the possession of the secured party be preserved or maintained;

b. In the proposal, proposes to accept collateral in full satisfaction of the obligation it secures; and

c. Does not receive a notification of objection authenticated by the debtor within 20 days after the proposal is sent.

(d) Effectiveness of notification. - To be effective under subdivision (a)(2) of this section, a notification of objection must be received by the secured party:

(1) In the case of a person to which the proposal was sent pursuant to G.S. 25-9-621, within 20 days after notification was sent to that person; and

(2) In other cases:

a. Within 20 days after the last notification was sent pursuant to G.S. 25-9-621; or

b. If a notification was not sent, before the debtor consents to the acceptance under subsection (c) of this section.

(e) Mandatory disposition of consumer goods. - A secured party that has taken possession of collateral shall dispose of the collateral pursuant to G.S. 25-9-610 within the time specified in subsection (f) of this section if:

(1) Sixty percent (60%) of the cash price has been paid in the case of a purchase-money security interest in consumer goods; or

(2) Sixty percent (60%) of the principal amount of the obligation secured has been paid in the case of a non-purchase-money security interest in consumer goods.

(f) Compliance with mandatory disposition requirement. - To comply with subsection (e) of this section, the secured party shall dispose of the collateral:

(1) Within 90 days after taking possession; or

(2) Within any longer period to which the debtor and all secondary obligors have agreed in an agreement to that effect entered into and authenticated after default.

(g) No partial satisfaction in consumer transaction. - In a consumer transaction, a secured party may not accept collateral in partial satisfaction of the obligation it secures. (1965, c. 700, s. 1; 1975, c. 862, s. 7; 2000-169, s. 1.)

§ 25-9-621. Notification of proposal to accept collateral.

(a) Persons to which proposal to be sent. - A secured party that desires to accept collateral in full or partial satisfaction of the obligation it secures shall send its proposal to:

(1) Any person from which the secured party has received, before the debtor consented to the acceptance, an authenticated notification of a claim of an interest in the collateral;

(2) Any other secured party or lienholder that, 10 days before the debtor consented to the acceptance, held a security interest in or other lien on the collateral perfected by the filing of a financing statement that:

a. Identified the collateral;

b. Was indexed under the debtor's name as of that date; and

c. Was filed in the office or offices in which to file a financing statement against the debtor covering the collateral as of that date; and

(3) Any other secured party that, 10 days before the debtor consented to the acceptance, held a security interest in the collateral perfected by compliance with a statute, regulation, or treaty described in G.S. 25-9-311(a).

(b) Proposal to be sent to secondary obligor in partial satisfaction. - A secured party that desires to accept collateral in partial satisfaction of the obligation it secures shall send its proposal to any secondary obligor in addition to the persons described in subsection (a) of this section. (1965, c. 700, s. 1; 1975, c. 862, s. 7; 2000-169, s. 1.)

§ 25-9-622. Effect of acceptance of collateral.

(a) Effect of acceptance. - A secured party's acceptance of collateral in full or partial satisfaction of the obligation it secures:

(1) Discharges the obligation to the extent consented to by the debtor;

(2) Transfers to the secured party all of a debtor's rights in the collateral;

(3) Discharges the security interest or agricultural lien that is the subject of the debtor's consent and any subordinate security interest or other subordinate lien; and

(4) Terminates any other subordinate interest.

(b) Discharge of subordinate interest notwithstanding noncompliance. - A subordinate interest is discharged or terminated under subsection (a) of this section, even if the secured party fails to comply with this Article. (2000-169, s. 1.)

§ 25-9-623. Right to redeem collateral.

(a) Persons that may redeem. - A debtor, any secondary obligor, or any other secured party or lienholder may redeem collateral.

(b) Requirements for redemption. - To redeem collateral, a person shall tender:

(1) Fulfillment of all obligations secured by the collateral; and

(2) The reasonable expenses and attorney's fees described in G.S. 25-9-615(a)(1).

(c) When redemption may occur. - A redemption may occur at any time before a secured party:

(1) Has collected collateral under G.S. 25-9-607;

(2) Has disposed of collateral or entered into a contract for its disposition under G.S. 25-9-610; or

(3) Has accepted collateral in full or partial satisfaction of the obligation it secures under G.S. 25-9-622. (1965, c. 700, s. 1; 1975, c. 862, s. 7; 2000-169, s. 1.)

§ 25-9-624. Waiver.

(a) Waiver of disposition notification. - A debtor or secondary obligor may waive the right to notification of disposition of collateral under G.S. 25-9-611 only by an agreement to that effect entered into and authenticated after default.

(b) Waiver of mandatory disposition. - A debtor may waive the right to require disposition of collateral under G.S. 25-9-620(e) only by an agreement to that effect entered into and authenticated after default.

(c) Waiver of redemption right. - Except in a consumer-goods transaction, a debtor or secondary obligor may waive the right to redeem collateral under G.S. 25-9-623 only by an agreement to that effect entered into and authenticated after default. (1965, c. 700, s. 1; 1975, c. 862, s. 7; 2000-169, s. 1.)

Subpart 2. Noncompliance with Article.

§ 25-9-625. Remedies for secured party's failure to comply with Article.

(a) Judicial orders concerning noncompliance. - If it is established that a secured party is not proceeding in accordance with this article, a court may order or restrain collection, enforcement, or disposition of collateral on appropriate terms and conditions.

(b) Damages for noncompliance. - Subject to subsections (c), (d), and (f) of this section, a person is liable for damages in the amount of any loss caused by a failure to comply with this Article. Loss caused by a failure to comply may include loss resulting from the debtor's inability to obtain, or increased costs of, alternative financing.

(c) Persons entitled to recover damages; statutory damages if collateral is consumer goods. - Except as otherwise provided in G.S. 25-9-628:

(1) A person that, at the time of the failure, was a debtor, was an obligor, or held a security interest in or other lien on the collateral may recover damages under subsection (b) of this section for its loss; and

(2) If the collateral is consumer goods, a person that was a debtor or a secondary obligor at the time a secured party failed to comply with this Part may recover for that failure in any event an amount not less than the credit service charge plus ten percent (10%) of the principal amount of the obligation or the time-price differential plus ten percent (10%) of the cash price.

(d) Recovery when deficiency eliminated or reduced. - A debtor whose deficiency is eliminated under G.S. 25-9-626 may recover damages for the loss of any surplus. However, a debtor or secondary obligor whose deficiency is eliminated or reduced under G.S. 25-9-626 may not otherwise recover under subsection (b) of this section for noncompliance with the provisions of this Part relating to collection, enforcement, disposition, or acceptance.

(e) Statutory damages: noncompliance with specified provisions. - In addition to any damages recoverable under subsection (b) of this section, the debtor, consumer obligor, or person named as a debtor in a filed record, as applicable, may recover five hundred dollars ($500.00) in each case from a person that:

(1) Fails to comply with G.S. 25-9-208;

(2) Fails to comply with G.S. 25-9-209;

(3) Files a record that the person is not entitled to file under G.S. 25-9-509(a);

(4) Fails to cause the secured party of record to file or send a termination statement as required by G.S. 25-9-513(a) or (c);

(5) Fails to comply with G.S. 25-9-616(b)(1) and whose failure is part of a pattern, or consistent with a practice, of noncompliance; or

(6) Fails to comply with G.S. 25-9-616(b)(2).

(f) Statutory damages: noncompliance with G.S. 25-9-210. - A debtor or consumer obligor may recover damages under subsection (b) of this section and, in addition, five hundred dollars ($500.00) in each case from a person that, without reasonable cause, fails to comply with a request under G.S. 25-9-210. A recipient of a request under G.S. 25-9-210 which never claimed an interest in the collateral or obligations that are the subject of a request under that section has a reasonable excuse for failure to comply with the request within the meaning of this subsection.

(g) Limitation of security interest: noncompliance with G.S. 25-9-210. - If a secured party fails to comply with a request regarding a list of collateral or a statement of account under G.S. 25-9-210, the secured party may claim a security interest only as shown in the list or statement included in the request as against a person that is reasonably misled by the failure. (1965, c. 700, s. 1; 1975, c. 862, s. 7; 2000-169, s. 1; 2012-70, s. 18.)

§ 25-9-626. Action in which deficiency or surplus is in issue.

(a) Applicable rules if amount of deficiency or surplus in issue. - In an action arising from a transaction, other than a consumer transaction, in which the amount of a deficiency or surplus is in issue, the following rules apply:

(1) A secured party need not prove compliance with the provisions of this Part relating to collection, enforcement, disposition, or acceptance unless the debtor or a secondary obligor places the secured party's compliance in issue.

(2) If the secured party's compliance is placed in issue, the secured party has the burden of establishing that the collection, enforcement, disposition, or acceptance was conducted in accordance with this Part.

(3) Except as otherwise provided in G.S. 25-9-628, if a secured party fails to prove that the collection, enforcement, disposition, or acceptance was conducted in accordance with the provisions of this Part relating to collection, enforcement, disposition, or acceptance, the liability of a debtor or a secondary obligor for a deficiency is limited to an amount by which the sum of the secured obligation, expenses, and attorney's fees exceeds the greater of:

    a. The proceeds of the collection, enforcement, disposition, or acceptance; or

    b. The amount of proceeds that would have been realized had the noncomplying secured party proceeded in accordance with the provisions of this Part relating to collection, enforcement, disposition, or acceptance.

(4) For purposes of sub-subdivision (a)(3)b. of this section, the amount of proceeds that would have been realized is equal to the sum of the secured obligation, expenses, and attorney's fees unless the secured party proves that the amount is less than that sum.

(5) If a deficiency or surplus is calculated under G.S. 25-9-615(f), the debtor or obligor has the burden of establishing that the amount of proceeds of the disposition is significantly below the range of prices that a complying disposition to a person other than the secured party, a person related to the secured party, or a secondary obligor would have brought.

(b) Nonconsumer transactions; no inference. - The limitation of the rules in subsection (a) of this section to transactions other than consumer transactions is intended to leave to the court the determination of the proper rules in consumer transactions. The court may not infer from that limitation the nature of the proper rule in consumer transactions and may continue to apply established approaches. (2000-169, s. 1.)

§ 25-9-627. Determination of whether conduct was commercially reasonable.

(a) Greater amount obtainable under other circumstances; no preclusion of commercial reasonableness. - The fact that a greater amount could have been obtained by a collection, enforcement, disposition, or acceptance at a different time or in a different method from that selected by the secured party is not of itself sufficient to preclude the secured party from establishing that the collection, enforcement, disposition, or acceptance was made in a commercially reasonable manner.

(b) Dispositions that are commercially reasonable. - A disposition of collateral is made in a commercially reasonable manner if the disposition is made:

(1) In the usual manner on any recognized market;

(2) At the price current in any recognized market at the time of the disposition; or

(3) Otherwise in conformity with reasonable commercial practices among dealers in the type of property that was the subject of the disposition.

(c) Approval by court or on behalf of creditors. - A collection, enforcement, disposition, or acceptance is commercially reasonable if it has been approved:

(1) In a judicial proceeding;

(2) By a bona fide creditors' committee;

(3) By a representative of creditors; or

(4) By an assignee for the benefit of creditors.

(d) Approval under subsection (c) of this section not necessary; absence of approval has no effect. - Approval under subsection (c) of this section need not be obtained, and lack of approval does not mean that the collection, enforcement, disposition, or acceptance is not commercially reasonable. (1965, c. 700, s. 1; 1975, c. 862, s. 7; 2000-169, s. 1.)

§ 25-9-628. Nonliability and limitation on liability of secured party; liability of secondary obligor.

(a)   Limitation of liability of secured party for noncompliance with Article. - Unless a secured party knows that a person is a debtor or obligor, knows the identity of the person, and knows how to communicate with the person:

(1)   The secured party is not liable to the person, or to a secured party or lienholder that has filed a financing statement against the person, for failure to comply with this Article; and

(2)   The secured party's failure to comply with this Article does not affect the liability of the person for a deficiency.

(b)   Limitation of liability based on status as secured party. - A secured party is not liable because of its status as secured party:

(1)   To a person that is a debtor or obligor, unless the secured party knows:

a.   That the person is a debtor or obligor;

b.   The identity of the person; and

c.   How to communicate with the person; or

(2)   To a secured party or lienholder that has filed a financing statement against a person, unless the secured party knows:

a.   That the person is a debtor; and

b.   The identity of the person.

(c)   Limitation of liability if reasonable belief that transaction not a consumer-goods transaction or consumer transaction. - A secured party is not liable to any person, and a person's liability for a deficiency is not affected, because of any act or omission arising out of the secured party's reasonable belief that a transaction is not a consumer-goods transaction or a consumer transaction or that goods are not consumer goods, if the secured party's belief is based on its reasonable reliance on:

(1) A debtor's representation concerning the purpose for which collateral was to be used, acquired, or held; or

(2) An obligor's representation concerning the purpose for which a secured obligation was incurred.

(d) Limitation of liability for statutory damages. - A secured party is not liable to any person under G.S. 25-9-625(c)(2) for its failure to comply with G.S. 25-9-616.

(e) Limitation of multiple liability for statutory damages. - A secured party is not liable under G.S. 25-9-625(c)(2) more than once with respect to any one secured obligation. (2000-169, s. 1.)

Part 7.

TRANSITION.

§ 25-9-701. Effective date.

This act takes effect on July 1, 2001. References in this Part to "this act" refer to PARTS I, II, and III of the session law by which this Part is added to Article 9 of Chapter 25 of the General Statutes. References in this Part to "former Article 9" are to Article 9 of Chapter 25 of the General Statutes as in effect immediately before July 1, 2001. (2000-169, s. 1.)

§ 25-9-702. Savings clause.

(a) Pre-effective-date transactions or liens. - Except as otherwise provided in this Part, this act applies to a transaction or lien within its scope, even if the transaction or lien was entered into or created before July 1, 2001.

(b) Continuing validity. - Except as otherwise provided in subsection (c) of this section and G.S. 25-9-703 through G.S. 25-9-709:

(1) Transactions and liens that were not governed by former Article 9, were validly entered into or created before July 1, 2001, and would be subject to this act if they had been entered into or created after July 1, 2001, and the rights, duties, and interests flowing from those transactions and liens remain valid after July 1, 2001; and

(2) The transactions and liens described in subdivision (1) of this subsection may be terminated, completed, consummated, and enforced as required or permitted by this act or by the law that otherwise would apply if this act had not taken effect.

(c) Pre-effective-date proceedings. - This act does not affect an action, case, or proceeding commenced before July 1, 2001.

(d) Special rule for certain governmental transactions. - Notwithstanding any other provision of this act, security interests that were excluded under former Article 9 pursuant to former G.S. 25-9-104(e) or as to which the filing requirements of former Article 9 did not apply pursuant to former G.S. 25-9-302(6), and which are effective prior to July 1, 2001, but for which the applicable requirements for creation, perfection, or enforceability under this act are not satisfied on July 1, 2001, shall nonetheless be treated as valid, enforceable, and perfected security interests under this act for the duration of those security interests. (2000-169, s. 1; 2001-218, s. 4.)

§ 25-9-703. Security interest perfected before effective date.

(a) Continuing priority over lien creditor: perfection requirements satisfied. - A security interest that is enforceable immediately before July 1, 2001 and would have priority over the rights of a person that becomes a lien creditor at that time is a perfected security interest under this act if, on July 1, 2001, the applicable requirements for enforceability and perfection under this act are satisfied without further action.

(b) Continuing priority over lien creditor: perfection requirements not satisfied. - Except as otherwise provided in G.S. 25-9-705, if, immediately before July 1, 2001, a security interest is enforceable and would have priority over the rights of a person that becomes a lien creditor at that time, but the applicable requirements for enforceability or perfection under this act are not satisfied on July 1, 2001, the security interest:

(1) Is a perfected security interest for one year after July 1, 2001;

(2) Remains enforceable thereafter only if the security interest becomes enforceable under G.S. 25-9-203 before the year expires; and

(3) Remains perfected thereafter only if the applicable requirements for perfection under this act are satisfied before the year expires. (2000-169, s. 1.)

§ 25-9-704. Security interest unperfected before effective date.

A security interest that is enforceable immediately before July 1, 2001 but which would be subordinate to the rights of a person that becomes a lien creditor at that time:

(1) Remains an enforceable security interest for one year after July 1, 2001;

(2) Remains enforceable thereafter if the security interest becomes enforceable under G.S. 25-9-203 on July 1, 2001 or within one year thereafter; and

(3) Becomes perfected:

a. Without further action, on July 1, 2001 if the applicable requirements for perfection under this act are satisfied before or at that time; or

b. When the applicable requirements for perfection are satisfied if the requirements are satisfied after that time. (2000-169, s. 1.)

§ 25-9-705. Effectiveness of action taken before effective date.

(a) Pre-effective-date action; one-year perfection period unless reperfected. - If action, other than the filing of a financing statement, is taken before July 1, 2001 and the action would have resulted in priority of a security interest over the rights of a person that becomes a lien creditor had the security interest become enforceable before July 1, 2001, the action is effective to perfect a security interest that attaches under this act within one year after July 1, 2001. An attached security interest becomes unperfected one year after July 1, 2001 unless the security interest becomes a perfected security interest under this act before the expiration of that period.

(b)   Pre-effective-date filing. - The filing of a financing statement before July 1, 2001 is effective to perfect a security interest to the extent the filing would satisfy the applicable requirements for perfection under this act.

(c)   Pre-effective-date filing in jurisdiction formerly governing perfection. - This act does not render ineffective an effective financing statement that, before July 1, 2001, is filed and satisfies the applicable requirements for perfection under the law of the jurisdiction governing perfection as provided in G.S. 25-9-103 of former Article 9. However, except as otherwise provided in subsections (d), (e), and (g) of this section and G.S. 25-9-706, the financing statement ceases to be effective at the earlier of:

(1)   The time the financing statement would have ceased to be effective under the law of the jurisdiction in which it is filed; or

(2)   June 30, 2006.

(d)   Continuation statement. - The filing of a continuation statement after July 1, 2001 does not continue the effectiveness of the financing statement filed before July 1, 2001. However, upon the timely filing of a continuation statement after July 1, 2001 and in accordance with the law of the jurisdiction governing perfection as provided in Part 3 of this Article, the effectiveness of a financing statement filed in the same office in that jurisdiction before July 1, 2001 continues for the period provided by the law of that jurisdiction.

(e)   Application of subdivision (c)(2) to transmitting utility financing statement. - Subdivision (c)(2) of this section applies to a financing statement that, before July 1, 2001, is filed against a transmitting utility and satisfies the applicable requirements for perfection under the law of the jurisdiction governing perfection as provided in G.S. 25-9-103 of former Article 9 only to the extent that Part 3 of this Article provides that the law of a jurisdiction other than the jurisdiction in which the financing statement is filed governs perfection of a security interest in collateral covered by the financing statement.

(f)   Application of Part 5. - A financing statement that includes a financing statement filed before July 1, 2001 and a continuation statement filed after July

1, 2001 is effective only to the extent that it satisfies the requirements of Part 5 of this Article for an initial financing statement.

(g) Inapplicability of subdivision (c)(2) to certain financing statements. - With respect to an effective financing statement that:

(1) Before July 1, 2001, was filed and satisfied the applicable requirements for perfection under the law of the jurisdiction governing perfection as provided in G.S. 25-9-103 of former Article 9,

(2) Would satisfy the applicable requirements for perfection under this act, and

(3) Was properly continued before July 1, 2001, such that the effectiveness of the financing statement would lapse after June 30, 2006, but before January 1, 2007, but for subdivision (c)(2) of this section,

subdivision (c)(2) of this section shall not apply to the financing statement and the filing of a continuation statement with respect to the financing statement is timely if the filing of the continuation statement occurs before the financing statement ceases to be effective and not before the earlier of (i) December 30, 2005, or (ii) six months before the effectiveness of the financing statement would lapse. (2000-169, s. 1; 2001-487, s. 15; 2006-11, s. 1.)

§ 25-9-706. When initial financing statement suffices to continue effectiveness of financing statement.

(a) Initial financing statement in lieu of continuation statement. - The filing of an initial financing statement in the office specified in G.S. 25-9-501 continues the effectiveness of a financing statement filed before July 1, 2001 if:

(1) The filing of an initial financing statement in that office would be effective to perfect a security interest under this act;

(2) The pre-effective-date financing statement was filed in an office in another state or another office in this State; and

(3) The initial financing statement satisfies subsection (c) of this section.

(b) Period of continued effectiveness. - The filing of an initial financing statement under subsection (a) of this section continues the effectiveness of the pre-effective-date financing statement:

(1) If the initial financing statement is filed before July 1, 2001, for the period provided in G.S. 25-9-403 of former Article 9 with respect to a financing statement; and

(2) If the initial financing statement is filed after July 1, 2001, for the period provided in G.S. 25-9-515 with respect to an initial financing statement.

(c) Requirement for initial financing statement under subsection (a). - To be effective for purposes of subsection (a) of this section, an initial financing statement must:

(1) Satisfy the requirements of Part 5 of this Article for an initial financing statement;

(2) Identify the pre-effective-date financing statement by indicating the office in which the financing statement was filed and providing the dates of filing and file numbers, if any, of the financing statement and of the most recent continuation statement filed with respect to the financing statement; and

(3) Indicate that the pre-effective-date financing statement remains effective. (2000-169, s. 1.)

§ 25-9-707. Amendment of pre-effective-date financing statement.

(a) "Pre-effective-date financing statement". - In this section, "pre-effective-date financing statement" means a financing statement filed before July 1, 2001.

(b) Applicable law. - After July 1, 2001, a person may add or delete collateral covered by, continue or terminate the effectiveness of, or otherwise amend the information provided in, a pre-effective-date financing statement only in accordance with the law of the jurisdiction governing perfection as provided in Part 3 of this Article. However, the effectiveness of a pre-effective-date financing statement also may be terminated in accordance with the law of the jurisdiction in which the financing statement is filed.

(c) Method of amending: general rule. - Except as otherwise provided in subsection (d) of this section, if the law of this State governs perfection of a security interest, the information in a pre-effective-date financing statement may be amended after July 1, 2001 only if:

(1) The pre-effective-date financing statement and an amendment are filed in the office specified in G.S. 25-9-501;

(2) An amendment is filed in the office specified in G.S. 25-9-501 concurrently with, or after the filing in that office of, an initial financing statement that satisfies G.S. 25-9-706(c); or

(3) An initial financing statement that provides the information as amended and satisfies G.S. 25-9-706(c) is filed in the office specified in G.S. 25-9-501.

(d) Method of amending: continuation. - If the law of this State governs perfection of a security interest, the effectiveness of a pre-effective-date financing statement may be continued only under G.S. 25-9-705(d) and (f) or G.S. 25-9-706.

(e) Method of amending: additional termination rule. - Whether or not the law of this State governs perfection of a security interest, the effectiveness of a pre-effective-date financing statement filed in this State may be terminated after July 1, 2001, by filing a termination statement in the office in which the pre-effective-date financing statement is filed, unless an initial financing statement that satisfies G.S. 25-9-706(c) has been filed in the office specified by the law of the jurisdiction governing perfection as provided in Part 3 of this Article as the office in which to file a financing statement. However, a termination statement shall not be filed under this section in the register of deeds office unless it is the office specified in G.S. 25-9-501.

(f) No additional fee. - No separate fee shall be charged for the filing or indexing of a concurrently filed termination statement under subdivision (c)(2) of this section. (2000-169, s. 1; 2001-231, s. 6.)

§ 25-9-708. Persons entitled to file initial financing statement or continuation statement.

A person may file an initial financing statement or a continuation statement under this Part if:

(1) The secured party of record authorizes the filing; and

(2) The filing is necessary under this Part:

a. To continue the effectiveness of a financing statement filed before July 1, 2001; or

b. To perfect or continue the perfection of a security interest. (2000-169, s. 1.)

§ 25-9-709. Priority.

(a) Law governing priority. - This act determines the priority of conflicting claims to collateral. However, if the relative priorities of the claims were established before July 1, 2001, former Article 9 determines priority.

(b) Priority if security interest becomes enforceable under G.S. 25-9-203. - For purposes of G.S. 25-9-322(a), the priority of a security interest that becomes enforceable under G.S. 25-9-203 dates from July 1, 2001 if the security interest is perfected under this act by the filing of a financing statement before July 1, 2001 which would not have been effective to perfect the security interest under former Article 9. This subsection does not apply to conflicting security interests each of which is perfected by the filing of such a financing statement. (2000-169, s. 1.)

§ 25-9-710. Special transitional provision for maintaining and searching local-filing office records.

(a) In this section:

(1) "Former-Article-9 records" means:

a. Financing statements and other records that have been filed in the local-filing office before July 1, 2001, and that are, or upon processing and indexing will be, reflected in the index maintained, as of June 30, 2001, by the local-filing office for financing statements and other records filed in the local-filing office before July 1, 2001; and

b.   The index as of June 30, 2001.

The term does not include records presented to a local-filing office for filing after June 30, 2001, whether or not the records relate to financing statements filed in the local-filing office before July 1, 2001.

(2)   "Local-filing office" means a filing office, other than the office of the Secretary of State, that is designated as the proper place to file a financing statement under G.S. 25-9-401(1) of former Article 9. The term applies only with respect to a record that covers a type of collateral as to which the filing office is designated in that section as the proper place to file.

(b)   A local-filing office must not accept for filing a record presented after June 30, 2001, whether or not the record relates to a financing statement filed in the local-filing office before July 1, 2001. This subsection does not apply, with respect to financing statements and other records, to a filing office in which mortgages or records of mortgages on real property are required to be filed or recorded, if:

(1)   The collateral is timber to be cut or as-extracted collateral; or

(2)   The record is or relates to a financing statement filed as a fixture and the collateral is goods that are or are to become fixtures.

(c)   Until July 1, 2008, each local-filing office must maintain all former-Article-9 records in accordance with former Article 9. A former-Article-9 record that is not reflected on the index maintained at June 30, 2001, by the local-filing office must be processed and indexed, and reflected on the index as of June 30, 2001, as soon as practicable but in any event no later than July 30, 2001.

(d)   Until at least June 30, 2008, each local-filing office must respond to requests for information with respect to former-Article-9 records relating to a debtor and issue certificates, in accordance with former Article 9. The fees charged for responding to requests for information relating to a debtor and issuing certificates with respect to former-Article-9 records must be the fees in effect under former Article 9 on June 30, 2001.

(e) After June 30, 2008, each local-filing office may remove and destroy, in accordance with any then applicable record retention law of this State, all former-Article-9 records, including the related index.

(f) Repealed by Session Laws 2001-231, s. 7. (2000-169, s. 1; 2001-231, s. 7.)

Article 10.

Effective Date and Repealer.

§ 25-10-101. Effective date.

This act shall become effective at midnight on June 30, 1967. It applies to transactions entered into and events occurring after that date. (1965, c. 700, s. 11.)

§ 25-10-102. Specific repealer; provision for transition.

(1) The following acts and all other acts and parts of acts inconsistent herewith are hereby repealed:

Uniform Negotiable Instruments Act, G.S. 25-1 through G.S. 25-199.

Uniform Warehouse Receipts Act, G.S. 27-1 through G.S. 27-53.

Uniform Bills of Lading Act, G.S. 21-1 through G.S. 21-41.

Uniform Stock Transfer Act, G.S. 55-75 through G.S. 55-98.

Uniform Trust Receipts Act, G.S. 45-46 through G.S. 45-66.

Agricultural liens for advances, G.S. 44-52 through G.S. 44-64.

Bank collections, G.S. 53-57 and 53-58.

Bulk sales, G.S. 39-23.

Factor's lien acts, G.S. 44-70 through G.S. 44-76.

Assignment of accounts receivable, G.S. 44-77 through G.S. 44-85.

(2) Transactions validly entered into before July 1, 1967, and the rights, duties and interests flowing from them remain valid thereafter and may be terminated, completed, consummated or enforced as required or permitted by any statute or other law amended or repealed by this act as though such repeal or amendment had not occurred. (1965, c. 700, s. 2.)

§ 25-10-103. General repealer.

Except as provided in the following section, all acts and parts of acts inconsistent with this act are hereby repealed. (1965, c. 700, s. 6.)

§ 25-10-104: Repealed by Session Laws 2006-112, s. 56, effective October 1, 2006.

§ 25-10-105. Repealed by Session Laws 1967, c. 562, s. 3.

§ 25-10-106. Covered transactions not subject to prior registration statutes.

Any security interest subject to article 9 of the Uniform Commercial Code and which is perfected by filing or otherwise under the Uniform Commercial Code, article 9, shall not be subject in any way to chapter 47 of the North Carolina General Statutes. (1965, c. 700, s. 4.)

§ 25-10-107. Repealed by Session Laws 1967, c. 562, s. 5.

Article 11.

1975 Amendatory Act - Effective Date and Transition Provisions.

§ 25-11-101: Repealed by Session Laws 2012-194, s. 11, effective July 17, 2012.

§ 25-11-101.1: Repealed by Session Laws 2012-194, s. 11, effective July 17, 2012.

§ 25-11-102: Repealed by Session Laws 2012-194, s. 11, effective July 17, 2012.

§ 25-11-103: Repealed by Session Laws 2012-194, s. 11, effective July 17, 2012.

§ 25-11-104: Repealed by Session Laws 2012-194, s. 11, effective July 17, 2012.

§ 25-11-105: Repealed by Session Laws 2012-194, s. 11, effective July 17, 2012.

§ 25-11-106: Repealed by Session Laws 2012-194, s. 11, effective July 17, 2012.

§ 25-11-107: Repealed by Session Laws 2012-194, s. 11, effective July 17, 2012.

§ 25-11-108: Repealed by Session Laws 2012-194, s. 11, effective July 17, 2012.

Vision Books Order Form

Fax Orders: 1-980-299-5965

Phone Orders: 1-704-898-0770

E-mail Orders: www.visionbooks.org

Mail Orders: Vision Books, LLC
P.O. Box 42406
Charlotte, NC 28215

Shipp To:
Name_____
Address_____
City_____State_____Zip_____
Phone_____Fax_____
Email_____@_____

Bill To: We can bill a third party on your behalf.
Name_____
Address_____
City_____State_____Zip_____
Phone____(_____)_____Fax_____
Email_____@_____

Pamphlet Number ($15.00 Each)	Qty	Total Cost
_____	_____	_____
_____	_____	_____
_____	_____	_____
_____	_____	_____
_____	_____	_____
_____	_____	_____
_____	_____	_____
_____	_____	_____
Full Volume Set 1-92	**92 Pamphlets**	**1,380.00**

Free Shipping Shipping & Handling on Full Volume Orders
Add $1.00 Shipping & Handling per pamphlet $_____

Total Cost $_____

Thank You for Your Support. Management!

DID YOU ENJOY THIS BOOK?

Vision Books would like to hear from you! If you or someone you know has been falsely imprisoned, we would like to hear your story. If the 'North Carolina Criminal Law and Procedure' has had an effect in your life or if you have suggestions, we would like to hear from you. Send your letters to:

Vision Books, LLC
Attn: Staff Writers
P.O. Box 42406
Charlotte, NC 28215
Email: staff@visionbooks.org

Order Additional Copies:

Fax Orders:	1-980-299-5965
Phone Orders:	1-704-898-0770
E-mail Orders:	www.visionbooks.org
Mail Orders:	Vision Books, LLC P.O. Box 42406 Charlotte, NC 28215

www.ingramcontent.com/pod-product-compliance
Lightning Source LLC
Chambersburg PA
CBHW051641170526
45167CB00001B/286